Money
Alchemy

GW00599641

Other books by Kiki Theo

Money Well – How to contain wealth
Wealth Journey – 9 Steps to a Wealthier You

www.moneyalchemy.com

Money
Alchemy

Into wealth & beyond

Kiki Theo

PENGUIN BOOKS

PENGUIN BOOKS

Published by the Penguin Group
Penguin Books (South Africa) (Pty) Ltd, 24 Sturdee Avenue, Rosebank, Johannesburg 2196,
South Africa
Penguin Group (USA) Inc, 375 Hudson Street, New York, New York 10014, USA
Penguin Group (Canada), 90 Eglinton Avenue East, Suite 700, Toronto, Ontario, Canada
M4P 2Y3 (a division of Pearson Penguin Canada Inc)
Penguin Books Ltd, 80 Strand, London WC2R 0RL, England
Penguin Ireland, 25 St Stephen's Green, Dublin 2, Ireland (a division of Penguin Books Ltd)
Penguin Group (Australia), 250 Camberwell Road, Camberwell, Victoria 3124, Australia (a
division of Pearson Australia Group Pty Ltd)
Penguin Books India Pvt Ltd, 11 Community Centre, Panchsheel Park, New Delhi – 110
017, India
Penguin Group (NZ), 67 Apollo Drive, Mairangi Bay, Auckland 1310, New Zealand (a
division of Pearson New Zealand Ltd)

Penguin Books (South Africa) (Pty) Ltd, Registered Offices:
24 Sturdee Avenue, Rosebank, Johannesburg 2196, South Africa

www.penguinbooks.co.za

First published by Penguin Books (South Africa) (Pty) Ltd 2008
This edition published 2010

Copyright © Kyriaki Theodosiadis 2008

ISBN 978 0 143 02672 3

Designed and typeset by Nix Design
Cover designed by Minette de Villiers
Printed and bound by Interpak Books, Pietermaritzburg

This book is not intended to provide personalised legal, accounting, financial, or investment
advice. Readers are encouraged to consult competent professionals with regard to matters
such as interpretation of law, proper accounting procedures, financial planning and investment
strategies. The author and the publisher specifically disclaim any liability, loss or risk which
is incurred in consequence, directly or indirectly, of the use and application of any contents
of this work. The author of this book does not dispense medical advice or prescribe the use
of any technique as a form of treatment for physical or medical problems without the advice
of a doctor, either directly or indirectly. The intent of the author is only to offer information of a
general nature to help you on your quest for emotional and spiritual well- being.

The matter lies before the eyes of all; everybody sees it, touches it, loves it, but knows it not. It is glorious and vile, precious and of small account, and is found everywhere ... But, to be brief, our Matter has as many names as there are things in this world; that is why the foolish know it not.

The Golden Tract

Alchemy is the art of manipulating life, and consciousness in matter, to help it evolve, or to solve problems of inner disharmonies.

Jean Dubuis

Contents

Chapter 10   Money Alchemy – Wealth Reflections

A Beginning

Introduction

A training manual for wealth

This is a training manual for the money making journey. When you train for a race you need to develop qualities other than speed. To become a champion you must develop hidden qualities – belief, perseverance, stamina, vision. You must eat differently, develop a new routine, take vitamins. In other words you must change. It is the same with money making.

To make more money you need to change. You need to change who you are, how you think, and act and feel. That is the subject of this book. It is about how and what you need to change in yourself to make more money.

Each chapter introduces a new way to look at money, and enters into deep processing that enables you to change core aspects of yourself in a deceptively simple way. This work will transform you organically, subtly, and powerfully, into someone who makes more money.

You will discover and release any illusionary ideas you may be holding of what it is to be wealthy, and in so doing you will reveal the wealthy you that you aspire to become. You will also set up the path of attainment of that wealthy you.

Creating wealth is a journey of becoming. You do not need more intelligence, or education, or social connection, or even money making skill, to create more wealth. All you need is the willingness to change and a very clear idea of who you want to become.

You may already know this. You may also know that money is energy, that like attracts like, and that you need to picture your goals with deep emotion in order to create your own reality. But what does this mean when you try to translate it into a money making strategy? How does it help you to create wealth? How does it change who you are?

Knowledge alone is not enough. To journey into wealth you need training. You need to develop hidden aspects of yourself. You need to move from theory into practice. The practice is not conventional. It is a process which is mysterious, awe-inspiring, hidden from conscious awareness – it is alchemy, just as the title suggests. This is a money making training manual that shows you how to change into someone who creates wealth. It works too.

To grow an oak tree, you must plant an acorn

This book will plant seeds, it will reconfigure your belief systems, it will drop pebbles into the pond of your consciousness, and it will cause a shift in the way you view money, yourself and the world around you. This will in turn change the way you behave, and that will change the way the world reacts to you in response. One day, a lot sooner than you imagine, there will be a very different you staring back at you in the mirror – a more connected you, a you that knows you *can*, a wealthy you, a you living a very different life from the one you are living now.

You will not be able to pinpoint exactly where the change started, or how it all came together. You will not be able to put it down to this process or that action, or that event. There will have been so many seemingly miraculous occurrences, synchronicities, things falling into place in your life quite effortlessly, that you will find the link back to this book you are holding in your hands right now nothing more than a tug in your mind. But the tug will certainly be there.

The effectiveness of this approach lies in its subtlety, simplicity and effortlessness. You do not have to do anything other than read this book, and do the processing contained in it, to set in motion a chain of events that will radically transform you and your life.

It is an organic process of becoming, set in motion by the intent which is projected from this book coupled with your intent, which you will set at the start. The process will be fuelled by the increased awareness and shift in perception which reading this book will initiate and cultivate, and by the processing which will reveal and transform key aspects of yourself on a very deep level.

It's like falling into water. The only thing you have to decide is to get in. Once you are in, you will most certainly get wet. Take the plunge! The water's warm.

It's just a jump to the left

To bridge money and energy is a journey. It is an alchemical transformation of the self. It represents the bridging of all the other polarities in life – matter and spirit, visible and non-visible, material and spiritual, body and soul. To integrate the two you need willingness, intent, and attention. That is all. It can be really simple.

Here is my intent and my wishes for your Money Alchemy Journey, as usually stated before one of my Alchemy of Money courses:

> 'It is my intent that reading this book will inspire you, refresh you, lighten you, align you with your purpose, and manifest wealth for you, in every way.
>
> May you grow, may you flourish and prosper beyond your wildest expectations.
>
> May all your dreams come true. May you fly!'

Kiki Theo

Let the journey begin! Good Luck!

My Story

There is only one thing you want to know about someone who writes a book on money making, and that is, have they actually made money themselves?

You want to know that this is a real person, who has lived in the real world, and has some scars to prove it. You want to be able to relate to this person, to the extent that you believe that if *they* could do it, then you can do it too.

The story of growth

My story is the story of an ordinary Greek girl, abandoned by her mother at the age of two, raised by an abusive stepmother, and left to deal with a bankrupt company at twenty-two after her husband went into a coma. It is the story of going from there, penniless and without education or background, to becoming a director and owner of a private fund management company responsible for the management of hundreds of millions for some of the wealthiest people in the country, which I ran for ten years before its successful sale.

I retired a multimillionaire at the age of thirty-nine. I have delivered wealth creation courses and money coaching to individuals and businesses for more than three years since then, and more recently I have devoted myself to writing about money and transformation.

In order to become wealthy, I had to change from a painfully withdrawn, sad, angry, resentful, heartbroken, depressed, broke victim of circumstance to who I am today – a winner.

Today, I am financially independent. I am married to a wonderful sculptor and have two beautiful children. We all have curly hair. My husband Shaun used to have long blond curls like our little girl Sasha, when we first met on a Greek island. His hair is shorter now, turning a little silver. Alex, our little boy, has dark curls like me. We live in a beach house overlooking Kalk Bay harbour.

We live a simple, contented life. We are happy. I have come a long way.

The story of transformation

My study of transformation began when I was nine and first explored yoga. Since then I have studied psychology and healing of every kind, with a focus on Jungian psychology, meditation, and ancient energetic transmutation.

I have, over the years, developed numerous techniques and processes of my own which I have used and tested in the business world and, more recently, in one-on-one financial coaching and on my Money Alchemy courses. All the processes contained in this book have been tried and tested with great success by participants in my courses for the past three years.

I have been completely focused on two things my whole life – money making, and transformation. I know how to make money and how to grow and run successful businesses. I have created wealth for myself and also for wealthy clients whose investments I have managed. I also know how to facilitate transformation.

The story of wealth

Wealth is a relative concept. It means different things to different people. I set out to become wealthy because I wanted freedom. I wanted to break the cycle of having to work in order to keep living. I wanted my life filled with assets, and no liabilities. I wanted to actually own my home and cars and investments. I wanted real, actual wealth; real cash in the bank – not credit facilities, loans and bonds. I wanted financial freedom, and I achieved it at the age of thirty-nine.

Apart from achieving financial independence for myself, my greatest qualification for money making is the combination of my working experiences. I have run businesses in fields as varied as power tools (at all of eighteen years), personal development, recruitment, life coaching, publishing, and investment management. Although these industries are totally unrelated, by applying a few basic principles and some solid plans and goals, I was able to turn each of them into a success.

It wasn't always easy; it wasn't all plain sailing. But the lessons born out of launching these ventures, more often than not without capital, and of overcoming fear and adversity, have been essential in providing the strength, optimism, and philosophy to enable me to look at money making objectively.

My greatest experience in money making comes from managing other people's money. For ten years I ran a private investment firm for wealthy individuals. It was not only the investment strategies that we applied that I learnt from. Working closely with our investors, who were some of the wealthiest people in the country at that time, gave me deep insight into their personal strategies and approach to money making as well as to life.

I found myself, at a relatively young age, in the unique position of not only being entrusted to manage the millions of my clients, but also of being exposed to their innermost thoughts and feelings. I was able to compare the individual approaches and psychology of hundreds of investors and observe how their attitude to wealth creation played out over time. Why is it, for instance, that two brothers can invest the same amount on the same day, yet only one creates enormous success, while the other continues to require financial assistance from the first?

My interest and involvement in transformation enabled me

to make these observations consciously. While in the process of creating wealth for myself and others, I was observing how and what I was doing, what was working and what was not. I was using the energetic approaches and transformational techniques that I learnt outside the workplace to grow my business and the wealth of my clients. I was also developing my own approach based on these experiences. I was formulating my own processes on how to cultivate the ability to create wealth.

I was in the business of making money out of making money. The more wealth I created for my clients, the more wealth I created for my company and for myself. This was a business which intimately connected me with money in every way. It was the perfect place for someone who planned to write and teach about money to be.

I have been blessed with wonderful mentors, amazing business partners and incredible staff and clients. I am grateful to them all.

Successfully selling my portfolio management company and retiring financially independent at thirty-nine was the culmination of all the life goals that I had set ten years earlier. I wrote these goals while sitting under a tree at a Buddhist retreat centre, relatively broke. I was living in a bachelor apartment at the time, driving a yellow beetle (the old kind, this was 1985). I decided I would pursue my lifelong urge to help others once I achieved financial independence.

My list of goals started with new duvet covers and a bedside lamp, progressed to a Mercedes sports and baby grand piano, and culminated with a fully paid up house and contents and a million in currency. I wrote in a fabric-covered book tied with a black satin ribbon. I still have it. I achieved all these goals and more, and I did it through changing myself, which is the subject of this book.

Your story

Two things I know for sure. No matter what your past or present circumstances, you can go from where you are to where you want to be with the help of the guidelines in this book. The other thing is this – if I could do it, you can definitely do it too. No exceptions.

The real story of this book is *your* story. It is your story of change and wealth creation that will be written on these pages. I am only a catalyst.

I wish you luck on your journey!

2

The Basics

Before you plant an acorn, be sure you want an oak tree (How to use this book)

1. Each chapter in this book is a self-contained subject and journey. Each journey builds from the previous one. As you progress through the book you will uncover deeper and deeper layers of yourself. The book is written like a spiral. It curves around in a circle, eventually curling into the centre. This is done for a reason, which you will understand at the end. You will see the connections, and start to put the pieces together as you get further and further into the chapters.

2. Do not allow the processing sections to stop you from reading further. If you simply read the whole book, without doing any processing, you will still derive benefit. However, you are urged to do all the processing, as it is on this that the major portion of your wealth training depends. You can also do the processing as many times as you like, as each session will yield different results.

3. This is the start of a new wealth journey, even if you are on a wealth journey already, or think you are on one.

4. Before you start, *set your intent.*

    An intent contains an implied commitment to, and a decision to act towards and achieve a want or desire. An intent is an act of focus and the application of will and action. If I say 'I want to go swimming', it could mean anything, but if I say 'I *intend* to go swimming', I am giving the definite impression that my mind is made up and I am on my way to the beach or pool, costume and towel already packed.

    So before you start reading this book, *set your intent. Do that now.*

Why are you reading this book? What are you hoping to learn, achieve?

What would need to happen in your life for you to know this book has produced results?

Be specific. Write a list if you need to.

Be specific. What do you want? And what do you *really* want? What do you need, right now? It may have little to do with money.

Narrow down your list to the three most important things. Then pick what draws you the most at the moment. It does not really matter what it is, or whether it is logical. Don't make this too important.

Be specific. Say 'I want ...' Then state this as an intent. State your intention:

I INTEND TO BE A MILLIONNAIRE
I INTEND TO MANIFEST MY OWN HOME
I INTEND TO CREATE A SUCCESSFUL AND PROFITABLE ORGANIC FARMING BUSINESS
I INTEND TO OWN A NEW CAR

Do not create an intent out of negating something. Rephrase any negative want. For example, instead of 'I want no debt' rather make it 'I want all my accounts in credit'. Don't make this big and heavy, or Very Important. Just create an intent which will act as beacon and goal, helping you gain maximum benefit from reading this book.

5. How much benefit you receive from reading this book, how great a shift takes place in your life, how effortlessly you transform, how smoothly you increase your wealth, depends on *your decision* to do so.

6. Decide now that this is a life-changing moment. Decide now that this is where your wealth makes a fast shift forward. Decide now that this is the book that will change everything!

7. Are you ready?

    If not, what do you need to do to be ready? What do you need to let go of? What do you need to say no to? What do you need to say yes to? Decide to do it. Do it. Do whatever you need to do to become ready for your wealth journey.

8. Are you willing?

    This is what real readiness is all about. Draw on your willingness to move forward and change. Draw on your willingness to go into the unknown and bring back the treasure.

9. Are you ready?

Alrighty then! (picture Jim Carrey here saying this …)

Before you plant an acorn, you need to dig a hole (About the processing)

The processing in this book aims to prepare the ground in which the new seeds introduced in each chapter will be sown. You are at the same time also sowing the seeds from which the new wealthy you will grow. The preparation of the ground is done through the processes of **free writing, drawing, symbolic acts, and the use of metaphor as symbol.**

All of these methods are specifically used so as to reduce as much interference from the logical mind as possible. They are also aimed at accessing aspects of yourself which are below the tip of the iceberg. In other words, the processing will help you to discover things about yourself which are not normally in your conscious awareness.

Trust the process. You may not understand why you are doing some of the things you have been asked to do. Some of the tasks set may seem positively strange or bizarre. Trust the process. The less you are able to rationalise about what you are doing the better. The processing is part of a process. Each section builds from the previous one. Every exercise is a small part of a whole, which will only become apparent later. Trust the process and flow with it.

There is no wrong way to do the processing. There is no wrong way to understand the prompts or questions. The prompts are open-ended for a reason. The prompts are 'vague' for a reason. Trust the process and believe that the way you understand and respond to these prompts is absolutely, exactly right for you at this time – because it is. On another day, when you repeat the exercises, you may understand and respond to a question in an entirely different way. The processing has been specifically designed to facilitate just that! These processes have also been worked and refined by taking participants' input into account, for more than three years – they are not just relevant prompts randomly thrown together.

The processes we will be using for wealth training are creative processes using the right side of the brain – in other words, the creative side. For those of you who are unfamiliar with this type of work, allow yourself to enter new areas of possibility. Allow yourself to discover a new language. Yes, even serious business people in suits can do this type of processing; you do not need to be an artist or a 'creative' person. Everyone is creative. And money making is a very creative art.

• **Free writing**

Free writing is writing by allowing whatever emerges to appear on the pages. You do not think about what to write, how to phrase it, or worry about grammar or punctuation. You merely allow your hand to write. Again, it is setting your intent before the start, which is key. The purpose behind all the writing is to discover the unknown, or the less obvious.

Gently remind yourself of this purpose before you begin to write. Keep it light, though.

Summarising whole paragraphs into one sentence at the end of an exercise after highlighting the most important parts can at first appear daunting, but it can be done. You are trying to get to the essence of what you are writing about. The summary does not need to be a logical conclusion derived from the sum total of your input. The summary is more a matter of asking yourself 'so what does all that really mean?' Or 'what is at the heart of all that I have written?' Again, allow the summary to surprise you.

Summarising in this way is also practice for honing your focus and intent. To create what you want you need to get specific, and you need to get to the point. Summarising practice helps you to do just that.

When doing the writing exercises:

- Write for the recommended time only – use a timer.

- Keep the pen moving, just write, don't think.

- Do not censor anything – you can burn the paper later.

- Begin with the prompt, if you become stuck, repeat the prompt.

- *Drawing*

Drawing is the same as free writing, except you are not using words, but marks on the paper. Allow what emerges to appear without censoring or thinking. Once again, you are trying to discover the unknown about yourself, using yet another language. You do not need any art skill to do these exercises. You are not required to draw anything 'real'. Just draw whatever comes. Give yourself permission to observe what arises with interest.

- Draw for the recommended time only – use a timer.

- Keep the crayons moving, just draw, don't think.

- Do not censor anything – you can burn the paper later.

- *Symbolic acts*

A symbolic act can take the form of a specially created ceremony or it can be a mundane or routine activity which you perform with the intent to create change.

Some people call symbolic acts rituals. Ceremony is a better word. Apart from the word 'ritual' being quite scary for most, because it conjures all things witchy, it is not correct to call a symbolic act a ritual. (Not even in a book with alchemy in its title.) A ritual is a series of acts performed in exactly the same way every time – for example, the ritual of marriage, or the christening of a child. A ceremony may become a ritual for you if you repeat it regularly, in the same way.

A symbolic act is a way to focus your intent. It is a powerful means of concentrating energy. The energy comes from your intent and from the act itself, and you are directing it towards a certain decision or outcome. Symbolic acts help us to pay attention. It is great to perform a ceremony at the start or end of something, as well as at a point of great change.

What you actually do in a symbolic act is not as important as your focus and intent. What matters is that the symbolism you are using has relevant meaning for you. For example, a snake has long been used as a symbol of healing and transformation by some. For most people, though, snakes are repulsive and to be feared. For those who fear snakes, carrying out a symbolic act for transformation involving snakes as symbol would be counterproductive.

When you take a mundane activity and turn it into a symbolic act, you are setting up new patterns in the world around you and you are practising living those new patterns. It is like doing dress rehearsals before a play. So, for example, you may decide to clear out your wardrobe with the intent of letting go of that which no longer serves you in your life. It is the intent and focus that you set at the start that transforms the mundane act into a symbolic act of transformation. A mundane act done with the proper focus and intent can be likened to a meditation. Certainly it will create new pathways in your life in ways that appear to be quite miraculous.

- In ceremonies, use symbols that you can relate to.
- Whether performing a ceremony, or a mundane act, keep the symbolic act simple.
- Focus your attention and intent.
- Keep it light.

- *Working with symbol*

A symbol is that which represents something by virtue of association, thought, or similar qualities. A symbol is not the same as a sign which is a literal representation. For example, white, lion, cross are symbols of purity, courage, Christianity. They are universal Western symbols. But symbol is also something very personal, different for everyone.

Words are the language of the rational and represent a certain type of thinking which is analytical, logical and realistic (unless you are free writing, that is). Symbol on the other hand is the language of a more creative type of thinking, intuitive, holistic, and deeply personal. When we integrate and align the two, we have much more creative potential at our disposal, much more energy and power.

A metaphor is the use of a name or description for something which is not literal. Metaphor relates to transference (which is the literal Greek translation). With metaphor, we are transferring meaning, we are transferring ideas and beliefs, and ultimately we are transferring energy, because everything is energy – but more on that later.

Metaphor can be likened to symbol and is useful in expanding our perspective on life. We can take a situation which may be quite difficult to understand or relate to and radically transform it both in our minds and in reality by viewing it as metaphor for something else.

Metaphor and symbol can give meaning in situations that are hard to grasp. They can lighten heaviness and create a shift. Proper use of metaphor and symbol can create new pathways of thought and action, releasing energy that can be used for the creation of our dreams. Through the use of metaphor and symbol we can discover our innermost dreams and the means through which to attain them.

• *Beware, there be dragons (a metaphor for 'what to be aware of when processing')*

   ⚬ *Dragons on the inside*

   Change is not always comfortable. The processing may tire you. You will need time and space to integrate the shifts this work will initiate. All sorts of emotions and physical symptoms may arise. Mostly, these will pass, if you allow the space and time. As you release old ways of being and thinking, your body may assist through the release of mucus – you may experience flu-like symptoms, or diarrhoea. This will pass.

   Emotions may also arise to be cleared. These are emotions that may be linked to the old patterns that you are releasing. You may feel angry, or depressed, or sad. These emotions too will pass, if you allow the time and space for this. Simply reminding yourself that this is part of the process of preparing new soil for the creation of greater wealth will be a great help to you at these times.

Whatever emotions arise, allow them to pass. Do not get attached to them, or involved with them. Do not try to analyse where they are from, and how they got there. Simply observe them and allow them to pass.

There is only one exception to this. If, in the course of this processing, you find yourself being emotionally drawn into any traumatic event from your past, you must stop. This is a highly unlikely scenario, given the subject matter of this work, and I have never encountered it. However, it is not impossible.

The purpose of this work is not to process traumatic events. Remind yourself of this before you start any processing. The purpose of the processing in this book is to train you for the money making journey.

Should you remember, or be reminded of some past trauma, please do not continue with the work that sparked this off. Stop. See a professional counsellor or therapist to deal with what has arisen and then continue. You can also skip to another section of work until you can see a professional. It is a highly unlikely scenario, but it is possible.

❧ Dragons on the outside

What is very, very likely, though, is that this work will change you. It will change how you view money and the world. This work will change your wealth profile for the better. That is unless you really, really resist and struggle and hold firmly and steadily on to the old (with both hands and feet). But I warn you, this will be a hard thing to do.

Because money is coming to get you, so why resist?

For some of the people who have done this work, there is a sudden or immediate improvement in their wealth – money starts to pour in, business rapidly expands, projects materialise. Have a look at the following examples taken (with permission) from the feedback forms of some of The Alchemy of Money weekend course participants:

Since the course, I have clarity, focus, power. I got 15 new requirements from clients from the time I started the course until today (a week later).

Business has literally been flowing in. Specifications and requests from clients are simply flowing in! – **Wanda Olsweski, Director and Owner, Taudata Consultants (Pty) Ltd**

After attending the Alchemy of Money weekend workshop, I set my intentions very clearly. I intended to earn what I am worth – which is a fortune – and I set a very definite intention to purchase another investment property by no later than the end of September (two months later). Well!! I have just been given a 50% increase on my basic salary and have been offered directorship by the Chinese, which is a miracle!! As for the property, we have just purchased a beautiful apartment in the Gardens. Thank you for the shift in mindset. Thank you for teaching me very basic tools to process my life at home. – **Lee Harcourt, Director**

I had a call from my broker telling me that a policy for R236 000 was maturing in November (two months later). I had forgotten all about it, so this was a great surprise! – **Belinda Kraus, Professional Musician**

For most, though, it is a more gradual process of becoming. A subtle change that slowly seeps into every area of their life, so that one day they discover they are in a totally different place in their lives, with a radically different view of money and money making than they had before.

Here is a letter from Mignon Lots, Managing Director of PeerPower, that illustrates the point:

Dear Kiki,

I promised you a testimonial – here it is :)

I did Kiki's money alchemy workshop about a year ago. I reorganised my understanding of what money meant to me and realised that I could have as much money as I wanted to make the difference I want to make, and that it does not mean I am a bad or greedy person. I realised that money is an enabler to my life the way electricity is, and I don't have a bunch of complex feelings about electricity!

I created a clear vision that money is possible for me. I have had the most abundant year of my life this last year. Money has started flowing in, in unexpected ways and from unexpected sources. I feel like I have relaxed and am in the flow, instead of worrying. Thank you, Kiki, for assisting me with these shifts, I am deeply grateful.

Good luck with your book – I'm sure it's going to be FABULOUS :)

Take care,

Mignon
Managing Director, PeerPower

Some of the changes this work will facilitate have nothing to do with money.

I have manifested many parking spaces. A 2 kg weight loss since the workshop, and the realisation of one of my biggest dreams – to reunite with my brother. – **Christine English, Tour Guide**

Life changing for me. It's not just about manifesting a certain figure in my bank account (done and growing). It's about a shift in mindset and a change in direction, I can feel the changes happening daily. It's like I'm taking off emotional clothing and feeling lighter every day. The work that is done inside of one's self is what is magical. This is powerful stuff, Kiki. The work you are doing will change lives. – **Laura Harris, Business Manager**

I needed to change my attitude to money, and I did. This work is about changing attitudes and becoming focused. It's definitely not only about money. – **Mike Laatz, Professional Musician**

Beware, this work will change you!

Before you dig a hole, you need a spade (Tools you will need for processing)

The processing you will be doing in this book requires the following tools:

- A large A4 Wealth Journey book that you can write in
- A pen
- Several pieces of large, blank, poster cardboard paper – A3 – white is best
- A box of nice crayons, pastels, coloured felt tip pens or coloured pencils, or the whole lot
- An egg-timer, or other type of timing device
- No logic

- No seriousness
- No correction
- No censoring
- No one ever to look at what you have done (unless you want it)
- An open mind

Give yourself time and space to do this work. Be aware that you may feel very tired after some of the processes. Take time to rest. Take time to integrate the shifts and changes.

After you plant your seeds, you need to water the soil (Reflection)

One of the most important aspects of any of these exercises is to reflect at the end.

That is not the same as analysing, psychoanalysing (even worse) or judging (worse still!).

Analysing is when your mind either tries to make sense of the situation, like 'how can I not contain my body?' or when it tries to overcompensate by reaching profound conclusions like 'this must be a metaphor for when I am beside myself'.

Psychoanalysing is when the mind does the above, wearing a psychologist's hat, like, 'I have been beside myself ever since my mother took away my bottle at age three.'

Judging is when you blame yourself (which can be done with or without the above) like, 'she took away my bottle because I ate too much, I still eat too much and that is why I am beside myself, because I can't fit into myself. I need to go on a diet!' None of these methods are useful. None are reflection.

Reflecting is when you allow the information to wash over you. You just observe what is.

You look at what is there, with an open and enquiring attitude, ready to discover something new, ready to be surprised. Whereas analysing is an event – it happens here and now, straight away – reflection is a process, and takes place over time. Allow time for the new to emerge.

After you plant your seeds, they need sunshine and light (Keep it light)

The most important requirement for this work is a light touch. Keep it light. Keep it fun.

Keep it magical. Keep focused on the light. And trust the process.

In conclusion …

To derive maximum use from this book state your specific intent for what you want to achieve at the start.

- Do the processing lightly, with attention and intention.
- There is no wrong way to do the processing. There is no wrong way to understand the instructions.
- When you free write or draw, allow undiscovered aspects of yourself and the subject you are exploring to emerge without censorship.
- When you are performing a symbolic act, use symbols that have meaning for you and keep it simple.
- Trust the process. Trust that it will produce the results you want.
- Keep it light, and have fun!

Good Luck!

3

The Foundations

Foundations I – Creating Money Alchemy

Riding the money carpet

Alchemy connects us not only with the magician within, but also with the ancient land of myth. It connects us to the lines of alchemists and magicians who transformed, not just as a means to an end, but also as a process of evolvement – as a journey towards the self.

Alchemy speaks of transformation. To transform means to transcend, to rise above, to enter another realm of reality. That is what alchemy conjures for us. It offers the possibility to become something else, someone else, to become something different, something more. Alchemy draws us into the world of possibilities and the world of imagination.

Money Alchemy is created when your ability to imagine is linked to your ability to believe, and both are infused with sheer enthusiasm. Money Alchemy is what happens when you align your goals, desires, and vision with the energy of money. When you start to see money from a new perspective (which this book will introduce), you will begin to relate to money differently. Once you put into motion some of the techniques and processes contained in this book, and you link that to a very clear intent, the flow to greater wealth in your life will open – both monetary wealth, and wealth in every sense of the word. This will happen easily, smoothly, almost effortlessly, as if by magic.

That is what Money Alchemy is all about. And you can do it. Not in a haphazard, unconscious way as everyone does from time to time, but in a conscious, directed, skilful way. You will practise creating new realities systematically, consciously and lightly. And you will become better at it, as time goes by, and as you practise. Tennis playing requires practise. Piano playing requires practise. Creating alchemy requires practise. Money making requires practise.

Money making practise does not involve budgeting, or balancing of cheque books. Money making practise involves creating new realities, dreaming, believing, and imagining. It involves getting specific about what you really want and taking the decision to get it. Money making practise is practise in breaking boundaries, honing daring, overcoming fear, cultivating outrageousness and nurturing courage. It's practise in changing our mind, expanding our range of possibilities, and being able to tolerate the discomfort that change will produce. Above all, money making practise is about a feeling. It's about finding and connecting with the feeling that we are hoping wealth will create for us. And the more we can tune into the frequency of that feeling, the more we attract it towards us.

Money Alchemy is about a magical mystery tour of transformation and wealth creation that will change your total net worth. It is a process which will occur easily, almost effortlessly as you shift your attention and focus, as you remember things you've always known, as you let go of accumulated debris and as you realise that when you drop one tiny little pebble into the pond of your consciousness, everything will change forever. And the first tiny little pebble is imagination.

Imagining is more than thought

To create a prosperous life, to birth a successful business, to bring a cherished dream into being, to become wealthy, you need, firstly and foremost, the ability to imagine.

Imagination is more important than knowledge, said Einstein. And indeed, without the ability to imagine, nothing can be achieved. Budgets and financial planning, goal setting and positive affirmations, strategising, and even financial input, will be of very limited use to you if you cannot believe and imagine.

Imagining is more than merely thought, and it is even more than creating a picture in your mind. Imagining involves the creation of a reality not yet born, and infusing it with such feeling, such colour, such passion, such vision and belief, that you cause it to come into being.

That is alchemy. What is truly magical, however, is that we all possess both the tools and the qualities we need to create this alchemy, right now. Yes, you do too!

Even when we think we have forgotten, we still know, deep down inside that we are magicians, alchemists, able to transform things, situations, life, ourselves, from one aspect to another. You know, in this very moment, that if you really, really wanted to, you could! Could what? Well, whatever you wanted. You know you could, if you really wanted to. Am I right? Of course I am!

You know you can be more. You know you can have more. Not just of life, but of yourself, of your own magnificence. You know that with just a little bit of help, with a bit of direction, you can become the person you really see yourself as, when no one else is looking! And the good news is:

YOU ABSOLUTELY CAN!

To make money, or to create anything for that matter, from a business to a wonderful piece of composition, you need to get into an alchemical space of magic. You need to stand in the I-believe-with-total-and-unshakeable-conviction-and-nothing-you-tell-me-will-make-a-difference-to-what-I-intend-to-do-here-because-I-know-I-can space. You need to know, like the magician within knows.

My partner and I started our fund management company during a bear market (that's when shares are generally going down). The economy was depressed, our competitors were not doing well, and some were in fact even going out of business. Most people we spoke to advised us against this 'very foolish notion' of starting a portfolio management company. There was much grave head shaking by bespectacled men driving much better cars (and with far healthier bank balances) than we who knew better. Our friends and family were not very encouraging either.

But we were filled with hope, faith and enthusiasm. We simply knew we could create a company that offered absolute service excellence coupled with extraordinary results. We simply knew we could wipe out all the competition. Never mind if some of them had been in business for many decades – that makes them complacent, we thought; our service is bound to be better. Never mind if some fund managers were rated as top of the field – that will motivate us to become the best, we said. Never mind if it was a bear market – that's when people really need management, we agreed. So the economy is down, there's only one way to go, and that is up!

I can honestly say that our conviction was such that there was no way anything or anyone could have stopped us. And so off we set, at 'the worst possible time', and started a business in an industry going through a really bad slump with enough money saved to set up the business and cover rent and staff salaries for only three short months.

And the business we created became a roaring success. That's standing in the I-believe-with-total-and-unshakeable-conviction-and-nothing-you-tell-me-will-make-a-difference-to-what-I-intend-to-do-here-because-I-know-I-can space!

You need to know, like the magician within knows.

The snow goose need not bathe to make itself white.
Neither need you do anything but be yourself.

Lau-tzu

Finding the magician within

The magician within knows, with unshakeable balance. This is not knowledge based on fact or reason, but the knowledge of faith and trust. It is knowledge based on beingness and alignment with this beingness. It is knowledge arising from our connection with the Divine within and around us.

The magician within is light-hearted. He likes to play, like a child. He loves to create, because he can. He is drawn to delightful and amazing plans. He loves a challenge – the bigger, the better. He is powerful and strong, yet he is light enough to fly above the mundane into the land of make-believe which is the future. And in that future, he can make your dreams come true.

We want happy endings. We want to believe. We want magic. We want to follow our dreams. We want to express the part of us that can create, the part of us that knows. We want to remember that YES! It is possible! I CAN! And we even want to move beyond that, to I WILL. We want to transform.

We want to transform from who we are to someone truly magnificent. We might know exactly who we want to become, or like many of the alchemists that came before us, we may only have a glimpse of what may appear at the other end of the cauldron. We may not know for sure what will emerge on the other end of our transformation process. It is truly an act of faith to move beyond the known towards the land of dreams, and that faith is the start of the alchemical process.

When my dreams come and fetch me

So we have alchemy and imagination and the wizard within and connecting to the part that knows I Can, and feeling what we imagine wealth will create. So where is the money in all of this, you may well ask? Well, it's like this. In a nutshell (do it to a beat):

Alchemy, Money and Me

Alchemy's about money and me
Connecting to a feeling, that's going to be
The future me, and how I feel
When I'm wealthy and fabulous, and if it is real

Enough to get my wizard excited
To get his heart pumping and his visions delighted,
Then all I need do is believe that it's true
Have faith and imagine all the things that I'll do

When I'm rich and I have all the stuff that I need
Nice house, fancy car, have it all, without greed
I can wake up each day with a smile on my face
Have my breakfast in bed, I can even be late!

I can help feed the poor, I can get some new breasts,
I will have so much fun, I will need a good rest
In my yacht, on a cruise, or my holiday home,
If I know where the future is, I will not roam
Through the maze of the rational mind, and what's more
If I know who I'll be, that will open the door
To a me that is better than ever before,

I will grow, and expand, I will take up my power
I will say what I want (every day in the shower),

I will feel what that feels like, as if I were there
I will laugh in the face of each one of my cares

Till my frequency soars into wealth and beyond
And my dreams come and fetch me to finish this song
In the back of a Cadillac, or maybe a yak,
I can have what I want –

Now how about that?

I think that about sums it up. (What, you were expecting something more serious in this book? Lighten up!)

First you must know what you want – you have to imagine it. Then, you have to feel what that feels like in your body. Then, if you believe it and you can feel it, you will have it.

How it will happen, is what you can never know. That is what the alchemy is about. Why most people don't get it, is that they are too busy trying to dictate the form and shape of the alchemy, instead of simply putting the ingredients into the cauldron of possibility, and trusting. Most don't even have a cauldron. (They think it's too witchy.)

First you have to imagine it. Then, you have to feel what that feels like. Then, if you believe it, and you feel it, you will have it. Don't ask how, just believe. That is the start of alchemy.

For those who believe, no proof is necessary.
For those who don't believe, no proof is possible

John & Lyn St Clair Thomas

Connecting with I Can (or How to Imagine)

Wealth Training Process

Set aside 15 minutes to dream and imagine. If you cannot do this now, just continue reading the book, you can always come back to it later.

There is no wrong way to do this, or any of the other processes in this book.

- Sit in a quiet room in a comfortable chair where you will be undisturbed for about 15 minutes
- Breathe in deeply to the count of 3, hold for 3 and breathe out for 3
- Depending on your breathing rate, you can use a count of 4 or 5 if you prefer
- Continue to breathe rhythmically for a few minutes (using any comfortable count) until your body and mind have settled
- Now relax each part of your body in turn, slowly from head to toe, by putting your attention on it, and saying 'relax', until you are totally relaxed and calm
- Think back to a time or moment when life felt fresh and new and full of potential
- Think back to a time when you could let your imagination roam free
- Think back to a time when you knew you could do anything
- Think back to a time when you believed
- (Each of these prompts could be a separate event or moment, or the same one)
- Enter that moment fully, reliving all sights and sounds, tastes, and sensations

- Feel how you felt, and feel that feeling now, expanding through your body
- Practise moving your attention to that part of the body and then moving away
- Practise turning on that feeling of *I Can*, of expansion, of yes-ness
- Keep connected to the feeling for as long as you can
- Return to the present when you are ready
- Ensure you are in the present by saying to yourself, 'It is (date) and I am here in (place, city, country). If you still do not feel grounded, touch the ground and all four walls around you, repeating the above. This is very important – do not miss this step!

The more you practise this exercise, the more proficient you will become at it. Everything arises from this simple task. Anything you want to create, including wealth, depends on your ability to find this channel on your dial. Once you are able to make this connection at will, practise each morning in your bath or shower. It will reap enormous benefits.

Bean by bean you fill up a sack
Greek proverb

Bubble, bubble, money is no trouble (to get)

In the previous exercise you made a connection with a part of you that knows you can. You have summoned the images and feelings of previous times when you created, felt good, and won. When you summon these images and feelings to you, you begin a process. The process works on many levels.

On the physical level, endorphins are released making you

feel good, and you want to feel good again. On the mental level, this explanation is serving to put your mind at rest that this is a rational, explainable thing going on here, so there is no need to panic … On the level below consciousness, you are presenting the mind with a vision of what you want. Your mind can then bring more of the same to you. Energetically, you are sending out a certain frequency of fresh, new, I can, yes-ness, which will attract more of the same to you.

This is like preparing the soil of your money garden. Once you have decided what you will plant in this soil, the alchemy can continue.

There is the story of a young boy who so wanted a bicycle. Every day he would imagine himself riding it down the road next to his house, every day he would imagine the wind blowing through his hair and the sunshine warm on his back as he rode his bicycle down the road. It was a red bicycle with a little bell, which he had seen in the shop window in town. He'd named his bike Henry, and every day he imagined shining it and cleaning it, before putting it away in the shed. He had no idea how he would get the bike because they were not a wealthy family, yet still he continued to imagine and he believed without a doubt that he would get it, despite what his parents said.

Finally, on Christmas day, he got dressed in his Sunday best and went out to wait for Henry to appear. And lo and behold, there it was! Wheeled down the road by Mr Carter, the wealthiest man in town. 'Henry!' shouted the little boy running towards the bike which had a big bright bow tied on it.

'You've brought me Henry!' he cried to the startled Mr Carter.

And do you imagine that the little boy got his bike after all? Of course he did!

That is alchemy.

Set your sights high, the higher the better.
Expect the most wonderful things to happen,
not in the future, but right now.

Be afraid of nothing. You have within you —
all wisdom, all power, all strength,
all understanding.

Eileen Caddy

Wealth Reflections

Creating Money Alchemy

- Alchemy is about transformation
- Making money is a process of transformation
- Money alchemy can transform your physical reality
- Money alchemy can transform you
- Alchemy is about creating magic
- To create magic you must believe
- To create magic you must be able to imagine
- To create magic you must trust
- Initiating alchemy is a skill
- Cultivating a skill requires practise
- Ignite money alchemy with imagination and enthusiasm
- Imagination and enthusiasm are a frequency, like a channel on a dial
- Alchemy is about connecting with the wizard within
- The wizard within is light-hearted and fun
- The wizard within knows s/he can
- You are the wizard within

The most beautiful thing we can experience is the mysterious.
It is the source of all true art and all science.
He to whom this emotion is a stranger,
who can no longer pause to wonder and stand rapt in awe,
is as good as dead: his eyes are closed.

Albert Einstein

Foundations II – Money as Energy

Here's looking at money

Mostly, we think that money is a mathematical, logical, physical, serious, intellectual, non-creative, non-spiritual, non-ecological, inhuman, maybe even dangerous, very important 'something' that we have to work for, slog after, desire, pretend we don't really want, crave, loathe, despise, feel torn about, think we don't understand, secretly want to possess, try to hoard, love to spend, hate to spend, use, abuse, covet, save, boast about quietly, watch all our lives, make decisions over, 'thing'.

We are encouraged, on the one hand, to make important life decisions based on the amount of financial security these generate. Like, 'get a decent job first, then you can paint'. And on the other hand we are warned that money 'does not buy happiness' and in fact may even be 'the root of all evil'. So, what is money then? And how do we go about getting it?

You may think you know, but do you? Because what you really think, deep down inside, will determine not only how you see money, but also how you behave towards it, and this will in turn influence how it reacts in return. In other words, how you look at money will affect how money looks at you. Here are a few prompts to uncover what you really think about money.

> *Money is congealed energy, and releasing*
> *it releases life's possibilities*
>
> Joseph Campbell

- Keep the pen moving, don't think, just write. Allow the pen to write.
- Write for 2 minutes on each prompt. Time this.

Discovering Money

Wealth Training Process

1. Money is …
2. The truth about money is …
3. What I like about money is …
4. What I dislike about money is …
5. I fear money, because …
6. When I think about money I feel …
7. The colour/taste/smell/texture/sound/shape of money is … (do each one separately)
8. What money thinks of me is …
9. If money was a person, it would be …

When you are finished, read through, highlighting any-thing important with a different coloured pen, or a high-lighter, then summarise all of the above into one sentence.

Free writing from prompts will become easier as you go along, but in case you've never tried this before, here's an example of a two-minute free write based on one of the prompts above:

> *The truth about money is … there are so many truths I don't know where to begin. And my 'money truth' might be differ-ent to someone else's. The truth about money is that less is definitely not more. Truly, money is something I deserve – if I*

work well and honestly, money is a fitting reward. The truth about money is that it's not going to come to me – it doesn't grow on trees. Or maybe it does, in a once-upon-a-time land that I need to go adventuring to find.

Depending on the degree of your abandon, this exercise should have released an 'aha' moment, something may have clicked somewhere in your heart or mind. In any event, a pebble has been dropped into the pond of your consciousness. Its ripples will continue to expand your mind, your understanding, and ultimately, your wealth. So what is money then, you may ask?

Putting on rose-coloured glasses

Firstly, we can say that money is important. Even for those who believe that money has no effect on them, money is important. Money provides the glasses through which we see the world. They can be grim, misty, grey glasses, or golden, rosy pink, multicoloured and clear.

It is with money that we have our closest relationship. It directs where and how we live, who we mix with, where we go to school, how we dress and what we wear, what we drive, where and if we go on holiday, who we meet, who we marry, how we deal with sickness, how much suffering we experience, and even how we die.

This is the actual reality of what money represents. Money has power, and we don't like that. We hate to face exactly how much power money has over us, and so we pretend it does not exist. Or we pretend it has no power over us at all. We say 'I don't really want lots of money', or we say 'if I had lots of money it would not be for me, it would be for the orphans'.

Once in a while, you have to take a break and visit yourself
Audrey Giorgi

What your mother wouldn't give for that Porsche!

But let's face it, wouldn't you love to be really, really wealthy? Wouldn't you just love to be able to spend whatever you wanted? Wouldn't you die for that outfit? Wouldn't you give your left arm for that Porsche? Go on, admit it! Okay, so you want to travel, and you're not into cars. Well, how about being able to take off for a year and go anywhere? First class? All right then, how about you have the money and power to release every single dolphin into the sea? Or build homes for each and every homeless person on the planet? How about that?

Because *that* is the kind of power that money represents!

Money is Potential

Money has power and money has potentiality. It can create a hospital for the sick, it can be used to build a palace, it can cause addiction and death, it can bring down countries and create wars, it can build cities and relieve poverty.

Money is amoral. (This is not the same as immoral.) It does not care how and where it is used, provided the proper channels of flow are in place, it will go anywhere. It can be used to create or to destroy empires. We see evidence of this all around us.

Money is energy. It is physical and non-physical, all at once. It is the coin and notes and it's the things the coin and notes will buy. Money is both wave and particle, like light, depending on how you look at it. Mostly, though, money is un-manifest potential, like all energy.

Money is Energy

As energy, money is subject to different rules. If we treat money as energy, then we need to behave differently towards it. When we treat money as energy, we are looking at something that flows. We are looking at something that is not quite solid, or static. It is something that can change form and shape. We are looking at pure potential. We are looking at money as something that is everywhere – all around. Money is everywhere because energy is everywhere, and money is energy.

When we acknowledge this, we realise that what we need to do with this money energy is to direct and shape it. That is, after all, what money making is. It is the art of shaping, of taking a potentiality, and turning it into a reality. That is why I talk of alchemy. Taking something in one form and turning it into another, is alchemy. It is a process of transformation. It is also the only thing you can do with energy, as it cannot be created or destroyed. If you remember your school science …
This changes everything!

When you truly understand that money is energy, you recognise that you have control and power over its creation. Money is no longer a solid, physical thing that is out there that you must try to acquire or grasp, and hold on to.

Money is part of the energy that is all around you. All you need to do is direct and contain it. You will see how later.

When you realise that money is energy, you set about 'acquiring' it in a totally different way. In fact, you no longer try to acquire it; rather, you set up the means to allow it to flow, and you create a container for it to flow into. Your container is your dream or vision. It is that car, or house, or pair of sunglasses, or liberated dolphin.

> *The obscure we see eventually.*
> *The completely obvious, it seems, takes longer*
> Edward R Murrow

Viewing money with the right eye

Recognising that money is energy is the act of proper naming. Correctly naming means seeing something for what it is. When you know what something is, then you can change it. You cannot change water into wine without knowing that it is water you are dealing with and wine that you want to change it into.

Giving something its proper name is an act of power. Seeing something as it is, is an act of bringing yourself into the present moment. There is great power in that also. When you stand fully in the present, you stand in your power. This means you are able to act authentically and produce results.

Where is the money? The money is in you!

If you really understand that money is energy, and that you are energy, then you understand that you are the money! There is no one who will give it to you, or can keep it from you. There is no one who will make it for you, or qualify you to receive it. There is nothing you need that you do not already have, in this moment, as you read this book, for making as much money as you want.

Because, you are, and have always been, the one who is the money! You are the money.

Say it!

I am the money! Where I go, the money goes also, because I am the money!

> *It isn't that they can't see the solution.*
> *It is that they can't see the problem*
>
> G K Chesterston

Exploring Money

Wealth Training Process

Exercises for a rainy afternoon (can also be done when the sun shines)

These processes will give you a deeper understanding of you and your relationship with money. Each time you write, the data you uncover will be different. Give yourself permission to discover things about yourself you never knew before. Allow what emerges to appear without censorship.

Writing tips

- Keep the pen moving, don't think, just write. Allow the pen to write.
- Write for 2 minutes on each prompt. Time this.

1. **Viewing money with the right brain (is *that* what it really looks like?)**
    a) Using a large piece of paper and coloured crayons of your choice, draw money. Yes, that is not a misprint, 'Draw money'. What does that mean? Just see what emerges. Draw for about 5 minutes.
    b) Then, while looking at your drawing, write about it.
    c) Turn the drawing upside down and write about that.
    d) Highlight the important bits, then summarise into one sentence.

2. **Writing the money tale (once upon a time there lived a wealthy prince I wanted to marry...)**
   a) Write your money autobiography, for 5 minutes.
   b) You can write it in the first or third person (as I or s/he).
   c) You can write it as a fairy tale or story beginning with 'once upon a time ...'
   d) Highlight the important bits, then summarise into one sentence.

3. **Money beliefs, quotes and anecdotes ('she said *money* would make you go blind')**
   a) Write a numbered list of your money beliefs. Write for 5 minutes.
   b) Read through, and mark the origin of each belief. Where did it come from? For example, mother/priest/girlfriend/incident with cookie jar
   c) Highlight the important bits, then summarise into one sentence.

4. **Money, Money, Money (what more can I say?)**
   Write for 2 minutes on each prompt.
   a) What I know about money is ...
   b) What I don't know about money is ...
   c) I am like money because ...
   d) Money came to me on a sultry, moonlit night, and ...
   e) Later, I saw the darker side of money ...

   Highlight the important bits, then summarise into one sentence.

Summarise all the previous sections into one sentence.

What do you think of money now?

Either do not attempt at all, or go through with it

Ovid

Wealth Reflections

Money as Energy

- Money is both physical and non physical
- Money is Energy
- Money is Potential
- Money flows
- Money is everywhere
- Money needs direction and containment
- You can direct the flow of money
- You can contain money
- You are energy
- You and money are made of the same stuff
- You are the money

Money as Journey

Where would you be if you had all the money in the world?

What is at the end of your money journey?

Wealth Attunement

Money as Journey

1

Making money is a journey
It is a journey of discovery
It is a journey to the self
It is a journey of expansion

2

Every journey has a beginning
At the start of a journey you must know where you are
Every journey has a destination
At the start of a journey you must know where you are going

3

If you don't know where you are,
you cannot get to where you are going

4

Knowing where you are,
means knowing who you are
Knowing where you are
means being in the present

5

You cannot begin a journey from the past
You cannot begin a journey from the future
It is only from the present that you can begin a journey

6

Your destination will draw you to your journey
Money will flow towards your destination
Your money destination is your goal
Your goal is the feeling of a new you

You are your money destination
You are the goal!

Do you know where you are? Do you know where you are going?

The only journey is the one within
Rainer Maria Rilke

The journey is at the end of your feet!

Money making is a journey. It is a journey to the self. It is a journey of discovery. It is a journey towards the destination of new self. Without a destination, there can be no journey.

The journey to wealth is an exciting one, it is like a quest. We set off armed only with our vision and our enthusiasm. We meet challenges and overcome monsters and demons. We cross treacherous terrain and grow, grow, grow, before we arrive at and capture our prize, our goal. Goal is important. Not goal as an object you acquire, but goal as the destination of a journey. A destination has a landscape, a feel, a sense, a feeling. A destination will change you. And that, after all, is what you are after, a new you.

Feel like a million dollars, and it's yours!

Think back to the last time you bought anything – a suit, a car, or even a new pen. Try to remember what you were thinking as you looked at this desired object. What picture did you have in your head? Your mind will tell you 'you were thinking you needed a new car' or 'you were thinking you had lost your pen and needed a new one', that is what your mind will tell you. And that information is definitely true, but it's from one dimension, the thinking dimension. The emotional dimension that motivated your purchase, the picture that you imagined of yourself wearing or driving or using the item, involved a connection with how that thing would make you feel. You were after a good feeling.

Whenever you buy anything, you are buying the way you think that thing is going to make you feel. This is in fact the first law of selling. Next time you buy something, stop for a moment and observe your inner dialogue and process. It's fascinating stuff!

Your money is where your heart is

So, making money as the destination of a journey is inextricably linked with a feeling and a new self that you expect to have achieved at the end of that journey. It is not really a house, or the money in the bank, or the new car, or the paid-up fees at the private school that you are after. What you want is the way these things are going to change you and the way you feel. And this desire for a new feeling and a new way of being will be different for everyone.

It is very important to understand this point. Successful wealth creation is based on this understanding. No one wants a new car, or a better house, or fabulous holidays. Yes, really, this is true. I will prove it to you. Remember the last time you were absolutely, besottedly, head over heels, madly in love with someone, in the first few days after you met him or her? Do you remember? Now tell me seriously that you gave two monkeys about anything else going on around you at that time!

'I would give it all up, for a single breath of her hair'

If someone had asked you in that moment to trade in that wonderful feeling for the world – a house, holiday, millions of dollars – would you have done it? (If your answer is 'yes', you are in for a fabulous surprise one day!)

For the rest of the romantics, you know you would have said no. Why? Because you were already feeling on top of the world and nothing else could better the feeling. Case closed. Ultimately, it is our heart that rules, and that is good news, because it is through the heart that we begin and end our journey.

In the movie 'City of Angels', Nicholas Cage, in his role as an angel, gives up his many powers, as well as immortality, to be with his beloved, acted by Meg Ryan. They only get to spend one day together before she suddenly and tragically dies. When he is asked by another angel if, knowing how things would turn out, he would do it all again, he replies: 'I would give up all of eternity for a single, only a single, breath of her hair.' Wow!

Shining light on the dark side of the moon

Making money is a journey of discovery of the self. Not only the superficial one or two dimensional self, it is also the discovery of the deeper self, the hidden, unexplored and unexpressed self, and the dark self. This is the self that contains all the magic. This is the self that will unlock all your treasures. This is the self that guards all wealth. The dark self is the twin self of your heart.

Facing and transforming the dark self is the greatest aim of money alchemy. This is the very real lead that you need to transform into gold. And we all have lead – lots of it. Jung said 'the greater the being, the greater the shadow'. Uncovering, facing and transforming our shadow is the main part of all the life journeys, and it is especially the case with the money journey.

Only the shallow know themselves

Oscar Wilde

As you grow, money grows

Money will provoke and activate every fear, every insecurity, and every shadow you possess. When you commit to a money journey, when you take the decision to take money as a teacher and to open wide your coffers and reveal your treasure, be ready! Money is a great teacher, one of the greatest, which is why money is at the core of so much on the planet as a whole as well as in our lives. Not only that, but as your money making journey helps you grow, so your shadow grows with you.

So money making has an in-built transformational component to it. It's really quite fabulous (if you maintain a sense of humour ...) The more your money grows, the more you grow. That is the best part of the journey! I know you are keen to get started!

So let's find out where you are.

Paradise is where I am

Voltaire

I am here, at the centre of my being!

Where are you? This is a very profound question as it is so closely linked to 'who are you?' There is also no quick or easy way to answer the question. For the purpose of this exercise, we will keep it fairly simple, though you may access pretty deep and profound insights if you allow yourself to write with abandon (a pen or pencil will also do).

You can take this exercise as often as you like, your answers will always be different. You can also make up your own prompts.

- Keep the pen moving, don't think, just write. Allow the pen to write.
- Write for 2 minutes on each prompt. Time this.

Finding Your Elusive Self

Wealth Training Process

1. I am …
2. I am not …
3. I am at a place in my life which is …
4. I am at a time in my life which is …
5. I am here because …
6. I would leave this place if …
7. The colour/taste/smell/texture/sound/shape of 'me here' is … (do each one for 2 minutes)
8. I got to this place in my life through …
9. I would not be here if …

When you are finished, read through, highlighting anything important with a different coloured pen or a highlighter, then summarise all of the above into one sentence. Do not analyse, ponder on, or become attached to what has emerged. Simply observe. Trust the process.

This is the beginning of your journey. Be interested to find out what follows!

> *I think what we are seeking is an experience of being alive,*
> *so that our life experiences on the*
> *purely physical plane, will have resonances*
> *with our innermost being and reality,*
> *so that we actually feel the rapture of being alive.*

Joseph Campbell

I finally put it all together, then I moved!

The first part of any journey is discovering where you are. Knowing where you are means clear vision and being in the present. Clear vision is a reality check. We all need one from time to time.

I found myself living in Cape Town after selling my business and starting a new, married life with children. I had back problems for some time, so did not exercise. After the birth of my daughter, a mere 18 months after my son, I was carrying some excess weight. Yet my mind had not caught up with all of this new reality.

My conversation was a long list of 'used to', and somehow, though I knew it was no longer true, some part of me believed and held on to this past picture of who I had been. 'I used to be super fit,' I would say. 'I used to do tai-chi, Jung, musicianship, Italian, fencing, sing opera, play piano,' I continued, depending on what the discussion was about. 'I used to wear a size 32,' I told the shop assistant when I was asked for my dress size. 'I used to be the director of a portfolio management company' is how I answered 'what do you do for a living?'

> *Just remain in the centre, watching.*
> *Then forget that you are there*
>
> Lau-tzu

And the more I said these things, the more I held on to this old, past picture of who I was and what I was doing, which was a lie. These things were no longer happening. I was no longer a size 32, I did not exercise, I was not in business. In fact, I was clearly not in present time.

One day, three years later, I realised this (you can become deluded for a lifetime, believe me, so three years is not that bad). So I did a reality re-adjustment. I wrote a long list of *what I do not do*. I do not do tai-chi. I do not sing opera. I do not wear a size 32. I do not own a portfolio management company. I am not a director. This is how I wrote.

It was hard. Hard to write the list, harder to look at, even harder to accept and let go. Ultimately it freed me up, it brought me into the present. It allowed me to make changes. I mean, how do you get fit when you are out of shape, if part of you believes you are still exercising five times a week? Once I had confronted reality, I could move on with my life. Today I can say I exercise three times a week, I do belly dancing, I am a writer and a mother and I wear a size 34.

When you've got to go, you've got to go!

Over time, we get to believe our own bullshit (or cowshit, if you're a girl). It's true. And there's no polite way of putting it. Bullshit is bullshit. (Or cowshit if you're a girl.) We say things like 'I'm not really interested in making lots of money'. And though this phrase may be a well used social mask, a shield, a crutch, or a veil, over time, and with much repetition, we begin to believe it.

Once we do that, it becomes difficult to change it, to act on it, or to remember the truth behind that statement, which may be that actually I yearn to travel (and I do need money for that), but otherwise I am not really interested in making lots of money. Often, that's what we are really saying, but we've lost the plot.

We need to see what is there. We need to see who is there in the mirror. We must look at what we really believe, at how we really are. Not with judgement or criticism, but simply observing. Seeing what is there. Just looking. Taking stock.

Reflect on where you are, right now in your life, in your path, in your journey, in your wealth creation programme, whatever that means to you. Meditation is useful for this. Observing the mind. Not identifying with it, just observing the thoughts that arise. In that same way you can observe yourself. Discover where you are. Take stock.

Are you still there, under that hat?

Observe yourself carefully but compassionately for three days. See what is there. Record your findings, and/or discuss with a trusted friend. Do not judge yourself. Make any changes you need to make as a result. Take any decisions you need to take. Keep it light and easy. No stress. No bullshit.

Just see, really see, what and who is there staring at you from the mirror.

> *Knowing others is wisdom,*
> *knowing yourself is enlightenment*
> Lau-tzu

At the very core of any change is simple attention. That is the beginning. The most profound and radical changes in life and in our consciousness begin with a simple single moment of truth – seeing something for what it is. That moment could be right now.

It is really as simple as that!

Reflection of this nature, which should become daily practice, brings us into the present. Being in the present is central to most spiritual practices as well as to many transformational approaches.

We need to come into the now, be in the now, be here now. Ask yourself, 'where am I, right now?' Wait for the answer.

Look around, observe yourself and get your bearings. It is easy to become lost in the stimulus which is constantly around us. We can become stuck in the past, or in the future, in planning, in worrying. When we do, we are no longer here, now. So take stock, without pressure. Do not concern yourself with the 'why' of the situation. Why am I stuck in the past, why am I worrying so much, what is causing this? This is a waste of time.

Simply acknowledge what is. State your intent to change. Take a decision. Be in present time. Decide you will be in the present. That is enough to make a change. Your power is in the present. Before you can go anywhere you must know where you are. All journeys start from 'here'.

> *The real voyage of discovery consists not in seeking new*
> *landscapes, but in having new eyes*
>
> Marcel Proust

The dark side of the mirror

Once, a very long time ago now, I was in a very dark place in my life. I had gone from creating my first fortune in my early twenties, complete with successful business, husband, house on an acre and gold 733i (the first in the country), to being relatively broke. This, after working day and night for two years to repay debt, seeing my husband in and out of mental homes after an assault and subsequent coma, and an emotional divorce, followed by betrayal by the new love in my life.

I remember looking at my face in the mirror one morning and wondering how I could look so normal when I felt so absolutely shattered inside. Fortunately, I had given up all recreational drink at that time (and we had been doing a lot of recreation up until then) or else this tale may not have had such a happy ending.

Fortunately, as I had been studying transformation in its many forms from a really young age, I recognised (even while in the depths of despair) that I was simply not in the present.

And so I began a two-fold daily practice. I did not think too hard about this, it just happened. The first part of my daily practice was to repeat to myself, like a mantra, 'this too shall pass', over and over again, especially when I was overcome by grief.

The second part was a process of getting myself into the present. Every day, many times a day, and especially when despair and hopelessness would gnaw away in my stomach, or descend like a dark cloud of lethargy over my very soul, I would say to myself, out loud: 'I am in my car, it is Tuesday, 17 July 1982. I am driving through Bedfordview. Everything is fine.' Or I would say: 'I am sitting in my chair. It is Saturday 21 August 1982. I see trees and the sky is blue. Everything is fine.' And so on. Over and over and over again I would repeat where I was and what I was seeing around me until, slowly but surely, some years later, I began to realise that I was no longer suffering from the low grade depression that had been a part of my life in varying degrees for many years.

Over time, I was able to come into the present enough to create dreams of a new future and to slowly start a new life.

Before you can start your journey, you must come into the present.
Be here, now. It really is as simple as that!

What did your face look like before you were born?

Where you are is very closely linked to who you are. We wear many hats. We have many selves – all illusionary. Some are merely reflections of the picture that others hold of us. Have you noticed how, when someone thinks you are clumsy or incapable, you become even more so? In fact, experiments have shown that we behave in accordance with the expectations of others. Research in a school showed that not only did the teachers who were told a group of students had higher IQs than they actually had behave differently towards those students, but the students themselves started to score higher grades. What a wonderful tool this knowledge can be!

If you didn't see the tree falling, would it make noise?

Have you noticed how, when someone really loves you and thinks you are beautiful, you become more radiant and, yes, you look more beautiful. It is because someone is seeing and reflecting beauty and love on to you. They are holding up to you a version of how they see you. You, in turn, match the frequency of that image.

In the presence of some people we feel small, ugly, incapable (it's best to avoid these people). This is merely their view of us projected on to us. We see it, and depending on how grounded we are in who we are (or how we feel that day or that moment), we become it, we match that frequency to a greater or lesser extent.

What if we smashed the mirrors and saw our true face?

Elsa Gidlow

The point is, it's easy to lose the essence of who we are in the midst of so many projections, hats, masks, roles, selves. We are in fact all of these aspects, not just the one or the other. And yet we are greater than the sum of the parts.

Who are you, then, at the core of all of this? And who are you trying to become?

When he looked around, he was far from shore

You may be wondering what all this has to do with money and money making. Just to recap where we are for those who think they have lost the plot, or think I may have … This is where we are.

We are looking at money as a journey of transformation, of becoming, of expansion of the self as much as of wealth. We are looking at journey as having a point of departure, this being the here and now. We are saying that if you don't know where you are, you cannot get to where you are going, or to anywhere for that matter.

We have been looking at where you are and linking that to who you are. Because if I ask you 'where are you?' your reply will always begin with 'I am' and that is not just pure semantics. How this all links back to money, you will soon see.

Happy now? Okay.

First you have to feel it!

Who we (think) we are is closely linked to how we feel. That's the part we identify with the most. Do you feel wise, free, powerful, able, loving, joyous? Do you feel out of control, unattractive, dull, weak? Do you feel wealthy? What needs to happen for you to feel wealthy?

> *It takes a long time to become young*
> Pablo Picasso

You see, we can say something like this: I have debt, I have no money for treats or holidays, I'm overweight, my husband is having an affair (or my wife, if you are a man, (or woman)). I feel miserable and stressed. I feel poor. Therefore I am not wealthy.

Or we can say something like this: I have a credit balance in my bank account, I go overseas twice a year, I am slim and healthy, my husband loves me (or my wife, if you are a man (or woman)). I feel lucky and prosperous. Therefore I am wealthy.

For some it's: I rent a little cottage by the sea, I live modestly from my investments, I paint and write all day, my dog loves me, I have a few good friends, I have everything I need. I feel creative and content. Therefore I am wealthy.

And for others still, it's: I have given away everything I own. I live to serve God. I have food and a roof over my head. I feel blessed and divinely guided. I am wealthy.

What it means to be wealthy, which is how it feels to be wealthy, is different for everyone. Interestingly, you can have the exact same circumstances creating a totally different feeling in different people, depending on the situation.

For instance, the third example could be like this: 'I rent a little cottage by the sea, I live modestly from my investments, I paint and write all day, my dog loves me, I have a few good friends', but could end 'I feel lonely and deprived. I am not wealthy'.

Whereas the first example could read: I have debt (but it doesn't worry me, I have always lived this way), I have no money for treats or holidays (that's okay, I don't need that, I'm in love!), I'm overweight (which my new lover loves!), my husband is having an affair (or my wife, etc (etc)), (which is fantastic, as I am in love too!). I feel on top of the world. I am wealthy.

It is all a matter of how your circumstances make you feel. Wealth is not a measure or an amount. Wealth is a feeling.

It doesn't happen all at once.
You become. It takes a long time
Margery Williams

I remember the first time I realised that some of my clients, who were extremely wealthy, actually felt poor. This was quite a revelation for me. I observed how some of the less wealthy clients perceived themselves to be far wealthier than those who had enough wealth for many lifetimes.

What was the difference between the two? These were some of the wealthiest people in the country.

The difference was simply perception and, beneath that, a feeling. If you don't know what being wealthy feels like, you will never be wealthy! No matter how many millions you accumulate – this is a simple fact.

How does wealth feel to you?

So what does wealth mean to you? Who would you need to become, to be wealthy? What would you need to let go of, and what would you need to have, to be and to feel truly wealthy? Where are you hoping wealth will take you? And how do you expect that to make you feel?

The reason more people are not wealthy is because they do not know what being wealthy means. It is an abstract, like 'I would love to have lots of money'. What does that mean? You can't imagine what it means, and until you do, you won't have it. People become wealthy when they become specific. People become wealthy when they know what that means to them, not only in terms of the objects and amounts involved – the physical, concrete reality – but also in terms of how they want this wealth to make them feel.

I'd rather have roses on my table, than diamonds on my neck

Emma Goldman

What are you trying to feel? Who are you wanting to be? This is the destination of your journey. You'd best find out what it is, or else you will never get there. There is an old Persian proverb: 'I fear you will never reach Mecca, for you are on your way to Turkistan.' That is definitely the case both with money and with the money journey.

The good news is that once you know both where you are, and where you are going to, the rest is very easy. Really! Unfortunately we spend most of our lives in the space in between here and there. This is the space of trying to figure out 'how to get there'.

If only I'd known where I was going, I would have taken a plane

We say: I am not quite sure where I am, or where I am going, but I will sit here and try to work out if going by bus or by train is better. I will look at all the timetables, work out the routes, calculate the fares, and figure out how hard I have to work before I can afford those fares. (This is called a retirement plan.) I will bitch and moan every year that the fares are getting more expensive, less affordable.

Eventually I will say I can never afford to go on this journey. Not that I ever knew where it was that I was going. For if I did know where I was and where I was going, I may have discovered that it's near enough to walk – I never needed a bus or a train. If only I had known where I was, I would have taken that ride on a plane – if only I had known where I was going!

It's easy for you to say!

Actually, I speak from experience. Let me tell you a little story. Once long ago, I was living in a studio apartment in

Johannesburg, with a Siamese called Ming (he's not a part of the story, but he was a beautiful cat, and he would hate to be left out). I drove a Beetle (the old kind, this was 1986), and had a part-time telemarketing position, which developed into consulting for a portfolio management company. But that was later.

I worked on a commission only basis, and to supplement my sometimes non-existent earnings in the first few months, I sold wall coating door-to-door at night with my friend Basil. My father would regularly deliver groceries to me on a Saturday morning, which was just as well (though I naturally argued with him every time, insisting I did not need groceries).

Eight months later, I was on holiday at a Buddhist retreat centre in Nieu Bethesda in the Karoo. If ever you are in this part of the world do not miss it. The Buddhist retreat centre is no longer there, but Nieu Bethesda is one of those truly magical spots. It is a small village nestled between the mountains, where you will find tranquillity, beautiful skies, and a profound sense of rightness with the world.

I cannot remember what led up to me sitting under a beautiful old tree that day in the Karoo. But there I sat, writing down a list of goals in a fabric-covered book which ties with a black satin ribbon. I still have it. It was a long ambitious list. It started with new duvet covers and a bedside lamp, progressed to a Mercedes sports and baby grand piano and culminated in a house fully paid for, with all contents also fully paid for and 'a million in international currency'.

Then, I thought, I will be able to retire and help uplift the world. I will teach and write, and create. I gave myself five years to achieve those goals. It actually took me eleven to achieve everything on my list – and more. And look – indeed here I am, even as I write this, writing this book! (Is that tautology?)

To get where you want to go,
you must keep on keeping on
Norman Vincent Peale

It makes me feel like dancing!

The most significant part of this story is that I never had a clue how I was going to do it. I only had the feeling of what it would feel like. For me this feeling is golden and expanded, like I am about to leap up into the air with arms extended. It is the feeling of sunshine on my face in the countryside. Everything is fresh and full of possibility and anticipation. In my body, the feeling is in my heart. When I connect to it, it expands from my heart through my body, and makes my eyes widen and, finally, it puts a smile on my face. It makes me feel like dancing!

That is the feeling I held on to through all the years of growing from telemarketer, to investment consultant, to director of my own portfolio management company, to buying, in 1993, the original company I had worked for in 1986, to selling my company and retiring, financially independent, at the age of thirty-nine. In fact, to be quite honest, I forgot all about the list in my fabric-covered book for quite a few of those years. But the feeling, I always held on to.

It will take you a hundred years, if you try to work it out

There was no way I could have computed or calculated how to get from where I was when I wrote that list, to where I arrived when I had achieved everything on it. There is no financial planner, no matter how much of a genius, who could ever have given me a plan on how to do this. If I had calculated the cost of what I wanted, and compared that with my earnings back in

1986 (even taking into account the fact that my earnings were without ceiling, being commission based and growing, and my dad was feeding me), and then tried to work out how long it would take to earn what I wanted, I would have come up with something like a hundred years. In terms of pure investment returns I would have had to make astronomical gains, in something really risky and speculative. That's if I'd had the capital which, back then, I did not. In fact, if I had tried to work out how to get from where I was to where I wanted to be, I would have given up straight away. Because in terms of consensus reality, and in terms of where I was in my life at that time, what I wanted was impossible. But consensus reality is almost always wrong. And the really, really significant part is that you, too, can get exactly what you want – but first you must know what it is!

It is somewhere over the rainbow

Making money is a journey. It is a journey of creation, and a journey of becoming. Making money is not an event. It is an ongoing process of evolvement of self. This means you need to pack a lunch at least, if not a suitcase. And you need to find out both where you are and where you are going before you set out on your journey. This book is your map.

Do not think of making money as something that will happen one afternoon in between lunch and tea time. And then you just carry on with life as you know it. It is not like that. Making money will change you, and displace you. So be ready to become a new you in a new place. Who is that 'you' that you want to become? What does that 'you' feel like? Where is that wealthy you living? Deep down inside you know, and that space is your destination.

The reason more people do not make more money is fear of

travel. They want to stay where they are. They want to remain who they are. They fear change. Not only that, but often they don't know who or where they are or who or where they want to be.

> *Listen. Make a way for yourself inside yourself.*
> *Stop looking in the other way of looking*
>
> Rumi

Will I have to change my hairstyle?

Many people think that making money means getting this 'thing' and putting it 'somewhere', 'sometime', 'maybe'. 'I'm not too sure what this money thing looks like. I'm a bit afraid of it – does it bite?… I'm not sure where we'll put it – does it need house training? – is it big? – will it fit in the lounge? … I don't have much time for this, really, I work very hard and I have a five-year plan and a budget – will it fit into that? On the other hand, I'm quite happy as I am, I would hate to miss my soapies, or have to change my hairstyle, so I'm not really sure, but it sounds like a good idea, and everyone says it's the thing to do and I would so love to be able to say I'm wealthy!'

It's true, think about it.

> *What we need is more people who specialise in the impossible*
>
> Theodore Roethke

Making money is a grand adventure

The journey of money making is a grand and exciting adventure. It is called life. Unless you have committed to a spiritual path as monk, nun or teacher and have your basic daily needs taken care of, you are on this journey already. You may be on an old

69

bus headed for Guatemala and you don't even know it, or you may want to upgrade from business to first class on your flight to Honolulu – it does not matter.

To have a great trip you must know you are on a journey. You must know where you are, as well as where you are going. Most importantly you must know what that feels like. The destination of your money journey is a new expanded you. So the question is not so much 'How much money do you want to make?', it's 'Who do you want to become?' And, more specifically, how do you want that to make you feel?

When you know where you are, and where you are going, and how you want to feel when you get there, your journey has begun.

> *Only the impossible is worth doing*
> Dr Akong Tulku Rinpoche

Looking in on Your Ideal Future

Wealth Training Process

This exercise is very useful. You can write it out, or do it in your mind's eye in daydream mode while sitting relaxed in a chair, or lying down on your bed. Doing both forms is best. This is an ongoing project, so you can keep working on it and refining it during those dull moments in traffic, in the shower, or during boring meetings. The more detail and emotion you can infuse into the picture the better.

- Imagine a day living your ideal future. Imagine yourself waking up in your bed. Look at the bedroom and describe it. Look at who is there with you. Get up and look in the mirror, see the face looking back at you and observe everything about it, including the way it feels, the energy it radiates. Look at what happens next. Notice your surroundings in as much detail as possible. See your day unfold slowly around you, as you watch. See, feel, and imagine.
- Repeat as often as you like, adjusting and refining details each time.
- Become familiar with, and embrace this you from the future.
- Get to know the hopes and aspirations of your future self.
- Allow the future to unfold.

Wealth Reflections

Money as Journey

- Making money is not an event
- Making money is a journey
- Making money is a process
- Making money is a destination

At the start of your money journey:
- You must know you are on a journey
- You must know where you are
- You must know where you are going

- To know where you are means to know who you are
- To know where you are going means to know who you want to become
- Who you want to become is a feeling
- That feeling is the destination of your money journey

- You are the source of your money journey
- You are the destination of your money journey
- You are the money journey

The only journey is the one within
Rainer Maria Rilke

5

Money as Process of Transformation

Who is the new you that you are trying to buy with your money?

Wealth Attunement

Money as Process of Transformation

1

Alchemy is transformation
Life is transformation
You are constantly transforming yourself
Money is a tool of transformation

2

Transformation is change
Transformation is changing the form of things
Everything is energy
Transformation is about changing the form of energy

3

You are the one who wants to change
You are the one wanting to transform
You want money to help you transform

4

To transform you must know what you are transforming from
To transform you must know what you are transforming to
To transform you must be willing to go into the unknown
To transform you must be ready to change

5

Making money will transform you
Making money will expand who you are
Money will help you to become your picture of wealthy

6

Who you want to become is linked to how this will feel
Money will take you to that feeling
Money will help you create a new you
Money will transform you into the you you have imagined

There are so many selves in everybody, and to explore and exploit just one is wrong, dead wrong

James Dickey

Transforming you

Alchemy is transformation. Life is transformation. We are in a constant process of transforming. And money is a tool for this transformation. We can even go as far as to say money is *the* tool of transformation, as it governs so much of what we do.

Whatever you do in life, you need money. There are a few exceptions. Even when you join an ashram, or become a nun, and rely on others to clothe and feed you, it takes money. As a result, money is closely linked with your path, and with the way you develop as a being in this life.

Now most of the time we want to deny this fact or make it a lie. We want to pretend that money has no influence on us whatsoever. We want to feel that we are independent of money, that money does not, and cannot affect us. This is not true. But while we believe it to be true, we cannot change it.

The reason we cannot change it is because before you can transform something, you must know what it is. To change water into wine, you must know that it is water that you want to change, and that it is wine you want to change it into.

Change your rose-coloured glasses

To change or improve your money situation you must first be able to see the current situation as it is. To see the current situation as it is, you must let go of outdated beliefs that no longer serve, such as 'I am too creative, spiritual, intelligent, to be wealthy'. You must remove any rose-coloured glasses that are an impediment to wealth creation such as: 'My lack of wealth is an indication of how brilliant a musician I really am, like all the greats before me.' You must look and see how things really stand in the wealth department. Look and see what is there. This also means seeing *who* is there – in this case, you.

We often hear people say (and sometimes we are those people) money doesn't interest me, money is not important, I don't really want lots of money. Then in the next breath they tell you they would love to take that trip to see their sister abroad or be able to afford a car that works properly, or have enough to live without debt or pay off their credit card, but they can't, because they cannot afford it.

What we are really saying when we say we don't want lots of money is: 'I don't want to change. I'm too scared to change. I'm comfortable here. I don't want to rock my boat.' Because transformation is about change, and change is frightening.

To head for new destinations, you must leave the shore

Change is frightening because it means letting go – letting go of the safe shore and moving towards foreign and unknown lands. It may mean letting go of destructive habits, or of what no longer serves. Perhaps it's my lover, or my wife, or my job. Perhaps it's letting go of my addiction to worry or cigarettes or blaming the world.

Sometimes it means letting go of a cherished belief system I have held on to my entire life – like I am too decent to make money or I am too creative or too spiritual to make money. Always, it's letting go of an old me, and making room for a new me. And that is frightening. It is frightening not only because I am not sure who I am about to transform into, but because I don't know whether everyone around me is going to like this new me. Will I still have friends? Will I still have a partner?

Will my partner still love me? What if I don't want him any more? What if she doesn't want me any more?

Letting go, changing, transforming, is made possible with money. With wealth, we can no longer hide behind our excuses. We can no longer pretend. We cannot say, 'well, I can't leave this situation, unpleasant as it may be, because I don't have any money'. We can no longer say, 'well, if I had a trainer and a dietician I would also be slim and healthy'.

> *When I grow up, I want to be a little boy*
>
> Joseph Heller

We will have no excuse for not creating that brilliant music, or wonderful painting, or writing that best-seller. We will have no reason not to meditate for hours every day. We will also have to stop being superior to those with money – we will no longer be able to be too good or too decent or too socially responsible or too creative or too spiritual to have money. We will no longer be special, with a special tale of woe. We will simply be rich, like all those other yobs. Maybe even filthy rich. Or disgustingly wealthy. Frightening thought, isn't it?

We avoid wealth, because we know it means change. Change of position, change of possessions and, most of all, change of self. We are afraid to change because we do not know who we will become, and because we identify being wealthy with certain characteristics which we will not own. We are afraid to change most of all because we know that to do that, we need to face who we are.

So let's take a little moment to contemplate your current view of being wealthy. You can reflect, honestly and truthfully about these questions. Writing adds a different dimension to these questions. For ideal results, do both reflection and writing. Your answers will change over time.

Being Wealthy

Wealth Training Process

1. Being wealthy means …
2. To be really wealthy I would have to be …
3. If I had lots of money I would need to become …
4. If I had lots of money I would need to change …
5. If I had lots of money I could no longer be …
6. If I was truly wealthy I could …
7. The person who would most dislike my being wealthy is …, because …
8. When I am very wealthy I will get rid of …
9. Before I can become wealthy, I need to let go of …

When finished, highlight anything important and then summarise into one sentence.

If you don't tell the truth about yourself,
you cannot tell it about other people

Virginia Woolf

The Wealthy

Wealth Training Process

1. The wealthiest person I know is …
2. S/he … is … because …
3. I think the very wealthy are …
4. To become extremely wealthy you need to …
5. You definitely cannot become very wealthy without
   …
6. When you are very wealthy, you have to …
7. What I dislike about the wealthy is …
8. What I envy about the very wealthy is …
9. List all the clichés, beliefs, and parables you have
   heard about wealth and the wealthy
10. Mark next to each one, its source – where did you
    first hear/decide this?

When finished, highlight anything important and then
summarise into one sentence..

I don't want to turn into a pumpkin …

If your picture of 'wealthy' is ambiguous or negative, you
will never want to transform into that. No matter how hard
you try to make money, if you think that wealthy means dis-
honest, materialistic, un-spiritual, manipulative, un-creative un-
ecological … well, you figure it out. This thinking is often on
the levels below consciousness. It needs to be ferreted out,
uncovered, faced up to, confronted, admitted – then changed.
This is self-knowledge. This is looking at yourself as you truly
are.

When we look at ourselves as we really are, we will see our

light as well as our darkness. When last did you really look at yourself as you really are, warts and all? I recommend a wonderful little book called *The Secret of the Shadow* by Debbie Ford in this regard.

We avoid looking at who we really are most of the time, because seeing who we really are means looking at our shadow. When we resist change what we are resisting is looking at, and subsequently transforming, our shadow. Yet it is through the transformation of our shadow that we can really grow.

What's hiding behind your lamp?

'Shadow', a term first coined by Carl J Jung, is anything that is kept out of the light. It is anything that is hidden, unconscious, un-owned. Shadow is what grows behind us, even as our light grows. Shadow is not always synonymous with dark side or negative. The shadow of the quality of timid is boldness. The shadow of harshness is tenderness. The shadow of poverty is wealth. Shadow is anything we are in the dark about, about ourselves. Our shadow represents the potential for our deepest transformation.

Shadow also encompasses the negative qualities in ourselves that we keep hidden away. Shadow is the parts of ourselves which we find unacceptable. It is those qualities which we are ashamed of. Yet shadow represents the part of ourselves which we can transform from lead into gold. There is little we can do with the fabulous parts of our nature which we are aware of. It is the dark, murky, messy bits that are the manure of our growth. As well as those parts of our magnificence which we are hiding.

We fear looking at our dark shadow because we want to be nice. We have been told we must be nice and good and well behaved in order for anyone to love us, and in order to reach heaven. We have mastered hiding our dark shadow side so well, we can no longer admit to being nasty.

While I was walking along the beach the other day, I overheard a woman saying to her young boy, 'I don't need to be nice, I'm your mother' … This puts a whole new angle on shadow viewing …

We do not want to face those parts of ourselves that are cruel or destructive. And the result of this is that we live a lie. We pretend. And after pretending for so long, we start to believe the lie, and we forget the truth. Then we project our shadow on to the outside world.

When we project our shadow we find that the world becomes a very hostile and unaccommodating place. People are not helpful. We find that we are not in control of our own destiny. Things happen which are 'out of our control'. Our shadow, left unattended for so long, grows and grows, and goes on the rampage. We now have wonderful excuses for why we are not getting what we want. We have reasons to explain why we cannot make as much money as we desire.

Each entered the forest at a point he, himself, had chose,
where it was darkest and there was no path
from *Quest for the Holy Grail*

It's not my fault he broke the cookie jar!

We become victims. We suffer from bad economy, retrench-ment, high or low interest rates, wars in foreign countries, or the lack of rain. Surely this cannot be my fault, we say. I am good and nice, I live a clean life, and I meditate. As we decline responsibility for our creations, so our power diminishes.

The more shadow or darkness we can see in others or in the world around us, the more we are in denial about our own shadow.

The more conspiracy theories we subscribe to, the bigger our shadow grows. The more critical we are of others, the more our shadow lurks.

What you resist, will persist

Resistance to change, which is resistance to shadow viewing and shadow transformation, is a key obstacle in money making. To make money means to change who you are. To do anything means to change who you are. To change who you are, you need to accept who you are – both sides of the coin, good and bad.

Now I know you are thinking what about those really nasty folk who make fortunes? They haven't transformed their shadow. And you are right, you do not need to totally transform your shadow before you can make lots of money. You don't need to have cleared all your 'stuff' or 'blocks'. Looking around the world, we realise that that is certainly not the case.

What we need to do is stop pretending that we have no shadow. We need to confront our shadow, acknowledge it and recognise the enormous potential involved in its transformation.

> *It is only with the heart that one can see rightly;*
> *what is essential is invisible to the eye*
>
> from *The Little Prince* by Antoine De Saint-Exupéry

We are not going to diverge here into issues of morality, or karma, or right and wrong – all of that is out of the scope of this book. I am merely pointing out that you do not, in fact, need to become free of neuroses or reach enlightenment before you can make money, which is great news – but you do need to face your shadow. In fact, the making of money will in itself provoke your shadow.

Looking at un-owned parts of ourselves is a lifetime journey.

Dealing with the shadow is a big subject. Confronting our shadow requires courage and imagination. It need not be an arduous journey, though. It can be a great relief, like removing a corset; it can be a grand adventure. It certainly will enrich your life.

As you start to own your shadow, you become the co-creator of your world. When you no longer need to project your shadow on to those around you, you are able to take responsibility for what you create, good and bad. Taking responsibility for things means you have the power to change them. When you are ready to do that, you are ready to manifest! You are ready to create whatever you want – money, a new life and, most importantly, a new you. Because that is the greatest gift that money has for us – money offers the possibility of personal transformation.

Tiny moves produce big results

Letting go of the old, changing, transforming, can be very difficult; it can also be really easy. All it takes is willingness. All it takes is a decision. We can let go of anything in an instant, no matter what it is, regardless of how long we have been holding on to it. It is just an instant, a moment in time, it's just changing direction, slightly. It's just a jump to the left. Tiny moves can produce big results.

> *Take your life in your own hands and what happens?*
> *No one to blame*
> Erica Jong

In a famous experiment, a very large object was completely covered with a sheet. Small peepholes were cut into the sheet at various points. People were positioned at each of these holes, and they then had to gather in groups to discuss what they had seen. Obviously, each person saw something completely different, depending on where they had been positioned.

Which peep hole are you seeing the world through?

Although it was not the objective of this experiment, to me this illustrates how everything around us can change through a very slight shift in our perception or viewpoint. Look through a different peephole and the whole of reality as you know it changes.

Major change, big transformation, is not about big life-changing events. It's not about ninety degree turns – very few people have many of those in their lifetime. It's about tiny adjustments – turning your head to the right or slightly to the left to gain a whole new perspective. Big change is not an event, it's a space you discover yourself in one day. It's the result of a process and of a journey of transformation.

The process of transformation begins by taking stock of who and where you are. Once you can really look at this quite clearly, you are ready to look at the creation of a new, 'improved', wealthy you.

Money is a mirror, it shows us who we are. Money is a magnifying glass, it makes us more of who we are. Money is a means of creating a new beingness, and that after all is what we are trying to do with money. We are trying to transform ourselves into a 'new me'.

You cannot blame the cookies

Many of us have a fear that money will make us into something that we are not. That money will somehow corrupt us. This is especially so if we are on a moral high ground. When we have spent our lives defending a viewpoint, such as that lots of money is only acquired through the destruction of our resources, and we are passionate about the protection of our resources, and we are now challenged with the thought of making more money …

well, you can see how that will create a problem. We will not want to become one of 'those' people.

However, money is a neutral, amoral energy. And though there is no doubt that the power that comes with money is seductive, and can most certainly be abused, I believe that it is not money that takes that decision to use or abuse – you do. It's like cookies. Not everyone eats a ton of them and becomes fat. And those who do cannot blame the cookies.

Once I was a rich man ...

What you *do* to become wealthy is your choice. Don't blame money for it. Don't use money as an excuse for not facing the shadow you project into the outside world. Don't let other people's choice of path put you off money. Money is neutral.

There are those who grow wealthy through the sales of arms, or drugs, or chemicals which pollute the planet. There are others who make a fortune out of doing the exact opposite – building clinics, creating beautiful art or music, or creating alternative forms of energy.

The choice of how to create money is a personal one. The choice of who to become when you have money is a personal one. The wealthy drug dealer decided to become a drug peddler long before he became wealthy. The person with an interest in alternative energy had this interest before making money in the field.

We seldom find the creators of alternative energy becoming arms dealers because they want to create wealth or because they are now wealthy. Though many of the big mafia lords 'go clean' and fund many worthy causes once they become wealthy enough – according to the movies, anyway – so perhaps we need to re-think 'money is the root of all evil'.

The point is, it is not money making that corrupts, as many

of us think. It is not money that decides how you will become wealthy or who you will transform into with your wealth.

So take a decision. Who do you want to become? What do you want money to transform you into? And what do you want to transform money into? That is really the question.

Making money is a process that will change you

So let's see where we are so far. We are looking at money as a process of transformation of self. We are saying that it is not money we are after, but a new sense of self. We have looked at resistance to change as a key component in wealth creation – we fear change because we fear looking at our shadow.

Shadow refers to the un-owned parts of ourselves, both good and bad. We have said that in order to change we need to look at who we are and where we are, and we need to acknowledge, if not transform, our shadow. We have also looked at our fear that money will turn us into someone we are not.

> *I am only one, but still I am one; I cannot do everything,*
> *but still I can do something;*
> *I will not refuse to do the something I can do*
>
> Helen Keller

When you look at the creation of a 'new-improved-future-wealthy you', you are looking not only at the way this you looks, or what this new you possesses, you are mainly looking at how this new you feels. And it is this feeling that will ultimately act as a magnet to attract not only the money you need to perform this transformation, but the transformation itself.

What you need to do is to connect with the feeling you want at the end of your money chain. You need to discover, and then practise feeling, what having money will do for you. What feeling are you trying to feel by being wealthy? Are you trying to feel secure, independent, relaxed? Are you looking for gracious living, or the freedom to be eccentric? What beingness are you wanting to experience? Do you want the experience of being the director of a corporation or the benefactor of an orphanage? Do you want to be remembered as the person who saved the planet by revolutionising transport, or do you simply want to be a great parent? What is the new wealthy you going to feel like? Do you want to feel what it's like to stand in front of your newly completed 'Caine Towers'? Do you want to feel what it's like to travel first class and be driven in a limo? Or do you want to experience diving the best sites in the world? It's all about a feeling. Find out what that feeling is. Find where that feeling is in your body, and practise turning it on and off at will.

The sooner you can feel wealthy, the sooner you can connect with being wealthy, the sooner you will have wealth. That's how it works.

Whatever happens, you can be absolutely sure that making money is a process that will change you. This change can be for better or for worse, for both you and the world around you. The choice is yours.

Wealth Reflections

Money as Process of Transformation

- Making money is a process of becoming
- Making money is a quest for changing self
- Wealth creation is a process of self-transformation
- Wealth is a means of creating a new you
- To transform self you must change
- To change you must let go
- To change you must see yourself as you are
- To change you must acknowledge your shadow
- To change you must know who you want to become
- Who you want to become means feeling in a certain way
- Money is a mirror
- Money will make you more of who you are
- Being wealthy is a feeling
- The feeling of being wealthy is different for everyone
- To become wealthy you must connect to that feeling
- To become wealthy, you must be wealthy

We are free to the point of choice.
Then the choice controls the chooser

Mary Crowley

Money as Potential

What is the great potential within you that money can unlock?

Wealth Attunement
Money as Potential

1

Money is potential
Without form, potential cannot flourish
Without form, money cannot accumulate or grow

2

You contain unlimited potential
Money can make potential manifest
For potential to manifest it needs form

3

Potential needs form to contain it
Money needs form to contain it
Your money container is your goal and destination

4

Your money container must carry your dreams and hopes
Your money container must hold your goals
Your money container must contain your future self
Without a container you cannot hold money

5

Your container must be strong and durable
Your container must not leak, and it must be expandable
Your container must be large enough to contain your potential

6

Your money container will draw you towards itself,
like the river is drawn towards the sea
Your money container will find the river of its attainment
and link it back to you
You are your money container

*The greatest problem is not that our aim is
too high and we do not reach it,
but that it is too low and we reach it'*

Michelangelo

It will grow as big as the pot

Bonsai is the art of stunting the growth of trees by regularly clipping the roots and branches. A miniature fig tree, for example, is kept tiny by being contained in a small, ornamental, shallow pot. The seed of the fig tree has all the potential of growing to a height of 30 metres (100 feet), but when it is not given a large enough container to expand in, it cannot fulfil its potential.

Goldfish will grow according to the size of the pond or fish tank they are in. The bigger the container, the larger they grow, and vice versa. Strangely, this also applies to crocodiles – and to money.

Money is sheer potentiality. It can become anything you want it to be. It is amorphous, diaphanous, invisible – it is energy, all around us, but unseen. Like the wind, it is a powerful force when concentrated. Like energy, it can do amazing things when mobilised. Money is not a static. It is not an object, or even a means to an end. It is not something you go and fetch, or acquire. Without form, money cannot exist, nor can it fulfil itself as potential.

You may find this new way of looking at money rather strange, but think of this: 'Only the most foolish of mice would hide in a cat's ear. But only the wisest of cats would think to look there' (Scott Love) That's called, in this context, a koan (it has various spellings), which is a way of short circuiting the mind so it can give you a break while it tries to figure out what this means!

The point is, you cannot hold on to money, you can only contain it, and this is also true of potential. And in order to contain money or potential, you need a container.

There is nothing of which every man is so afraid
as getting to know how enormously much he is capable of doing
and becoming

Søren Kierkegaard

Go with the flow!

Unless we create a container for money to flow into, where is it going to go? How will it translate itself from a potentiality into a reality? How will it take form? Money is an energy, a flow, a force, certainly something that is in motion, and in the process of becoming – it needs to be harnessed and contained, or we might find ourselves thinking it's not really there. (This is called the mentality of lack.)

How we contain money is reflected in how we contain other things in our lives – our dreams, hopes, and aspirations, our goals, our relationships, our vision, our humanity, our weight. Ultimately, how we contain money reflects our ability to have. And as our ability to have arises out of our ability to be, or who we are, we can say that how we contain money is how we contain our beingness. Our beingness is limitless, we have unlimited potential but we need to find it, direct it, and contain it. I wrote the following story to illustrate this point.

The Earthenware Bowl and the River of Gold

There once lived a man of modest means. He was hard working and good and he lived in a lovely house in the forest. His house was surrounded by a wall, which had an opening on the east side. Every morning, before the sun came up, gold would flow in from the opening in the wall, filling a small earthenware bowl that the man placed there every evening.

The man used the gold to buy seeds to grow vegetables and fruit. He bought corn and he made butter and cheese. He mended his house when this was needed and he tended his garden. He lived a simple life, but there was never time to rest or to enjoy the beautiful sunsets. He longed for a wife and a family. He yearned to see the world beyond the walls of his house.

But his work was long and hard, and every evening, quite exhausted, he carefully washed his small earthenware bowl and put it out at the opening on the east side of the wall, then went to sleep.

The bowl had been given to him by his father, who had been given it by *his* father before him. 'Look after this bowl my son, for this is your livelihood. As long as you take care of this bowl, you will never go hungry,' his father had said.

'It's a little small, Dad,' he had answered 'I could make a new bowl, bigger and stronger, decorated with auspicious symbols and designs.'

But his father had mocked him. 'Sheer foolishness, my boy, wild dreams! Stick with what works,' he had said.

And so it was that the river of gold that flowed just outside the house rose with the tides every evening and poured through the opening in the east side of the wall. It filled the little earthenware bowl many times over, the excess spilling out over the sides for many hours, to be absorbed back into the earth. When daylight came, the tide receded, leaving the little earthenware bowl full of gold. Just full enough to fill the bowl, just enough to meet the man's needs.

Find the river or widen the bowl?

That's really the question. (Not how come he did not see the river, or why was it rising at night, or why the river was full of gold. This is a parable, after all!)

We often try to find the river of gold. That's what we try to do when we go to the casino, or play the lottery. Sometimes our company is bought for a large sum of money, or our invention is snapped up by the Danish, or we inherit from that uncle – and lo and behold, we have found the river of gold!

Interestingly enough, most (though not all) of the people who suddenly acquire large sums of money quite rapidly revert to where they were before the gain. There is extensive research on this phenomenon.

We know what we are, not what we may become

Shakespeare

Directing the flow of the river

Why is this so? Quite simply, it's the inability to contain. Finding the river is not enough. For unless we can direct the flow of the river towards a destination, unless we can contain it, the river will continue to flow past us unseen. This is the river of money we are talking about. The river of unmanifest potential, pure energy, which is everywhere around us. We also need to ensure that our flow of money is not blocked, diverted or obstructed.

If we can direct this flow, we help the river to fulfil its potential, we direct it towards its goal. And once it arrives there safely, we contain this river of potential, of money, of dreams, of our unmanifest magnificence, in a wonderful expansive, magnificent container. And when we successfully do this, we realise that it is we who have journeyed along the river, it is we who have arrived at the destination, in fact it is we who are both the river and the container.

To contain more money, you need a bigger container

As for the container, it definitely needs to be large enough to contain our goal, it must also be built sturdily and have no leaks. It must be expandable, and easily accessed by the river. For if your money container is not large enough to contain money, you will find that no matter how much you earn, you will always be in the same place in the wealth department.

You may have had this experience already. Suddenly there is a windfall of some kind, or an increase in income and then, lo and behold, something needs repairing, or an unpaid bill emerges. Why? It is because you have not adjusted the size of your container to contain more. So the excess merely flows away. To contain more money, you need a bigger container. It's actually quite simple.

You must be the change you wish to see in the world

Mahatma Gandhi

What Do You Contain?

Wealth Training Process

The following exercises will help you to focus on the metaphor of container from many different angles. Allow yourself to learn about yourself. Permit yourself to reveal layers below the surface. Know that this new knowledge is yours to keep. You need not share it with anyone. No one is watching you write. No one will read what you write. Let rip!

(a) Drawing my container

- Set aside 10 minutes for this exercise
- Get a large sheet of blank paper (A4 or bigger) and a box of crayons
- Label the paper 'my container'
- For 3 minutes draw your container – don't think about this
- Then, looking at your drawing, write about it for 5 minutes
- Underline important words or phrases and summarise into a sentence
- Turn the picture upside down
- Write about what you see now – don't think about it
- Underline important words or phrases and summarise into a sentence
- Observe your container and, without judgement, see:
  - whether it is big or small
  - tall or short
  - what it is made of
  - are the walls thick or thin?
  - is there a firm base, is it supported?
  - is there a base at all?
  - is the opening at the top wide or narrow?
  - does it leak?

- Underline important words or phrases and summarise into a sentence.

(b) Containing my world

Using the prompts below, write for 2 minutes on each of the following:

(Keep your hand moving, repeat the prompt if you get stuck)

- I contain ....   I do not contain ....
- My body contains ...   My body does not contain ...
- My beliefs contain ...   My beliefs do not contain ...
- My thinking contains .. My thinking does not contain.
- My talents contain ...   My talents do not contain ....
- My skills contain .....   My skills do not contain ....
- My views contain ....   My views do not contain ....
- My heart contains ...   My heart does not contain .....
- My dreams contain ..   My dreams do not contain ....
- My goals contain .....   My goals do not contain ....
- My money contains ..   My money does not contain ...
- My vision contains ...   My vision does not contain........
- My life contains .....   My life does not contain ....
- My potential contains . My potential does not contain...

- Underline important words or phrases and summarise into a sentence.

(c) How my world contains me

Repeat all the above prompts, except the first, switched around to read:

- I contain my body ...   I do not contain my body ....
- I contain my beliefs .. I do not contain my beliefs ...... and so on

- Underline important words or phrases and summarise into a sentence.

> **Summarise the entire exercise (a,b, and c) into one sentence.**

Part **c** may sound a little strange, so here are some examples:

- '*I contain my body* within my spirit and in my consciousness. I contain my body in my home. I contain my body within fine clothes and I love it. It is a fine body, healthy and sturdy. It has been strong enough to bear two children after forty …' and so on.

- '*I do not contain my body* when I am tired and ratty and irritable. It falls apart with lots of noise and people. I do not contain my body well. It feels bulky and horrible when I get my periods, I do not want it, it holds me down. I do not contain my body when I sleep …' and so on.

What have you done?

In this exercise you have looked as yourself as a container of things and you have looked at how you contain various aspects of your life. You have also looked at how various aspects of your life contain you. You are beginning to consider money as something you need to contain, and you are examining the ways in which you have contained money up until this point. You are starting to play with the concept of creating a container for your money, and are looking at possibilities for this.

The new information will form new patterns, it will raise new questions in your mind over the next while. Be open to this too. Another pebble has been dropped into the pond of your consciousness.

Drinking from an empty cup

So, to recap. To contain something, we need a container. The container for our money is our goal or vision. Without this, we cannot hold on to our money. The container has to be durable, expandable and have no leaks. Though our container will change over time as we grow and develop, at any one moment in time our container must have a constant and definite shape. This is very important. A half cup, half plate, maybe a tumbler will keep spilling its contents, whereas a big spaghetti pot will not. Italians will be happy to hear this.

This means that we need to have a specific goal or vision, for it is this that will contain our wealth. It is our goal towards which we direct our energy and intention. Committing to a specific goal is not easy, as we do not always know what we want. And what we want is always linked to a feeling.

Having a specific goal creates internal tension. It commits us to a course of action, puts us on the line, presents the possibility of failure, creates the possibility for expansion, and puts up parameters of exclusion (… if this is my goal, then that, and that, is not) – all of which is challenging.

> *You must do the thing you think you cannot do*
>
> Eleanor Roosevelt

I'm not sure it's a cup, maybe it's a saucer

We generally try to avoid specifics. We try to avoid looking at our heart's desire, and instead opt for generalisations like 'wanting to make a lot of money', or 'wanting to be comfortable'. But because these generalisations have no form, they cannot successfully contain money, and money seldom flows towards them.

Your specific goal, or cause, is what will reformulate money from a mere potentiality into a reality. Your specific goal is what will give money form, enabling it to be contained. Without a goal, without form, money remains an intangible possibility, a potential with no possibility of actualisation. You are the vehicle through which money can manifest.

A saucer? But it's got handles!

What does this mean in terms of money? Well, I do a whole weekend course on the subject of containing money, as it's a rather large subject. Here, we are looking at money as potential requiring a container. So I will introduce the key concepts of 'containing money' for you to consider and reflect upon, without entering into great detail on each. You can explore this subject in detail in my next book, *The Money Well* ™ – *How to contain the money in your life*.

For now, let's begin by looking at this container a little more closely. What makes a container is, firstly, the walls that differentiate the inside from the outside. Without those walls we would have a plate (or something). The walls refer to parameter, boundaries, restriction – a tricky subject, without a doubt.

We are looking not only at walls thick enough to hold in contents, but at walls that will not crumble under pressure. We want sturdy walls that are at the same time flexible. They must be flexible enough to change shape when we need to create something new. They must be flexible enough to expand without breaking or leaking. The strength of your walls also represents the sincerity of your intent and of your purpose.

How strong are your boundaries? What are your parameters in life and in money making? These are very broad questions to reflect upon, which will reveal fascinating information to you about your life as well as your new money container metaphor.

Get thee behind me, Satan

Fund management, like many other industries, can get dirty. In the eighties, professional companies were not allowed to advertise. Telemarketing teams would set appointments with prospective clients, whose names were sourced from share registers, and consultants would go out and sell portfolio management.

In an industry where share prices can be as fickle as the weather, a fund management company's client list was (and probably still is) worth many times its weight in gold.

In those days consultants were not as stringently regulated as they are today. And there were those consultants who would go to prospective clients making outrageous promises, running down competitors, telling outright lies, and generally getting business any which way they could. Not only were there consultants who operated in this way, there were fund management companies who ran their businesses this way too.

One such company acquired through dirty means the client list of a company we had just purchased. And even as we were going out to meet our 'new clients' and show them our past returns and impress upon them how we were going to take care of them and improve their portfolios, so these other nasty folk were running around trying to steal our clients through any means they could. Now we had paid a lot of money for our client list, which kept diminishing by the day.

It was unjust and unfair. It was dirty and underhand and made me absolutely furious. And it was then that the little horny creature with a tail made its appearance, in the form of a call that I will never forget.

It was one of the admin staff from one of the stockbrokers who knew of our plight. She said, 'I know what these guys have been doing. It's disgusting and unacceptable. Do you want to get your own back? I have a little list here I can let you have

…' She was offering us the client list of the company who were stealing our clients as a gesture of friendship!

Well, what do you think we did? Should I leave you in suspense with that one till the end of the book? More importantly, though, what would you have done? And you had better know the answer to that question off pat, fast and without hesitation. Because if you don't know exactly where your boundaries stand then, yes, money may well get you into trouble.

Where your boundaries are has absolutely nothing to do with circumstances. You either lie, or you don't. You either steal, or you don't. There are no buts to the decision. And this certainty of where you stand creates firm and solid boundaries in your container. And without solid and firm boundaries your container will not stand the test of time.

No, we did not for a minute contemplate taking that client list. We simply laughed and said 'get thee behind me, Satan'! And if it happened today or next year or in ten years' time, my answer would be the same. There is no doubt in my mind about that. And I know that the same is true for my then business partner.

It's not so much a question of morality, or of being good. It's simply a question of being true to yourself. It's a question of knowing what you are and what you are not prepared to do, and being prepared to put it to the test.

I don't want that. *This* is what I want!

The walls of your container are created through your choice. This is the choice of destination. It is the choice of container as goal. It is the decision to pursue *this* goal. It is a definite move away from 'making lots of money', 'being comfortable' or 'having enough'. It is the moment when you say:

'THIS IS WHAT I WANT!'

Not that, not this, but *THIS*. Have you ever watched how direct and specific children are? They say, 'I want *this* biscuit.' And they are never put off their course, no matter what. They will continue to demand the biscuit until they get it. They will not compromise.

The walls of your money container represent a decision and a selection, with no compromise. This is your goal, with full sensaround colour and feeling.

In the second instance, the walls represent the principle of exclusion and inclusion. What will you have in your container, and what will be outside? What forms part of your new reality with money? What do you want? And, most importantly, what will you let go of, what will you leave behind?

The thickness of the walls represents your boundaries with the world. Your own personal space boundaries. How you interact with others and how you allow them to interact with you. If the walls are too thin they will not stand. If they are too thick, nothing will come through, and it will be difficult to make changes as you develop.

Thin walls relate to having too little separation between you and the world. It is the syndrome of allowing everyone else's opinion and point of view and reality of the world to cloud or even obliterate your own. When this happens, you find that the walls of your container will not stand, your dream will not stand. You will allow the opinion of those-others–who–know-better to override your decision to start a business, or to go to Java to photograph the fire bird and, lo and behold, without walls, there is no container, so that's the end of that.

On the other hand, if your walls are so thick that you cannot dance with life, with your dream, with others around you, you will find that your container walls will not be flexible enough to accommodate a sudden rush of gold coming your way. They will simply keep it out, or crumble under the pressure.

Create firm walls. Not too thick and not too thin. Flexible walls that can dance and breathe with the flow of life and money.

Which lines will you cross to make money?

Parameters and restrictions also relate to your principles, ethics, code of honour. Literally, we are looking at which lines you are prepared to cross to reach your new horizons. It is really useful to know these things, for then you need never fear having to 'sell your soul to the devil' in order to achieve your aims. It is unnecessary to do so.

You can make money as honestly or as dishonestly as you like – you really do have that choice. Money itself is amoral (that's not the same as immoral, look it up) you are the one with higher consciousness, you are the one with choice and free will. You can make a choice on how you want to make money and what you are and are not prepared to compromise to do so. You have both the right, and the ability to do this. Exercise it.

To contain money is to contain magic

When you work with the concept of a container you will soon discover that how you contain money is reflected in how you contain other things in your life, and vice versa. How do you, and more importantly, do you, contain your enthusiasm, your joy, your fun, your laughter, your creativity, for example? Do you contain your dreams? Do you contain your potential?

To contain money is to contain magic. The magic is not in figures, or budgets, or retirement plans – if it was, would you be reading this book? The magic of money lies in creation, in fulfilling dreams, in connecting with your potential and finding a way to contain it and to manifest it.

The diffrense from a person and an angel is easy.
Most of an angel is in the inside and
most of a person is on the outside.

from Mister God this is Anna by 'Fynn'

Money is sheer potentiality, just like you. Can you catch the wind? Can you find the starlight? Yes and no. You need to acknowledge money's potentiality. Then, you need to create a really beautiful container. A container which is so alluring, so captivating, that the wind, or the starlight, or the money is drawn to occupy it. A truly magnificent container will beg to be filled.

Find your container. Build it beautifully, in magnificent detail. Make the walls firm and strong, but supple. Infuse your container with all the joy and thrill and wonder of finding yourself standing before it, full and overflowing. Then sit back and relax, as the pathway towards your destination unfolds, almost effortlessly.

This is money alchemy.

Containing Magic

Wealth Training Process

Reflections for a rainy afternoon

Write about, reflect upon, contemplate the following:
- If you had all the money in the world, what would you like to do?
- And then what would you have? (continue asking this 7x)
- What is your earliest memory of your ideal future/ profession?
- What do you really, really want to do, really?

- If you had a container, what would it be?
- What would you have inside and outside your container?
- What is your container made of?
- What is your potential? How do you contain it?
- What is your dream? How do you contain it?
- Make a wish list of everything you want. Be specific. Don't be shy.
- What do you really want?

Cherish every wish in your heart,
however trivial it may seem.
One day these trivial wishes will lead you to God.

from *The Way of the Wizard* by Deepak Chopra

Wealth Reflections

Money as Potential

- Money is potential
- Potential needs direction, form and containment
- Your goal is your money destination
- To contain money you need a container
- Your container is your goal
- Your money container must be specific
- Your container represents your choice of destination or goal
- The container walls represent boundaries and parameters
- The container walls must be strong, yet flexible
- Money will be drawn to fill your container
- You must expand your container as your money needs expand
- You contain the money
- You contain many aspects of your life
- Your ability to contain will determine what is contained
- Your ability to contain reflects your ability to be
- You must increase your beingness to increase your container
- You are your money container
- You are the potential unfolding

Undoubtedly, we become what we envisage
Claude M Bristol

7

Money as Relationship

Who is the money in your life? Do you have a good relationship with them?

If money was in an intimate relationship with you, how would it describe you?

Which of your relationships does your relationship with money mirror?

Wealth Attunement
Money as Relationship

1

Everything exists by virtue of relationship
Everything is connected
Everything is Energy

2

Your relationship to something affects that thing
When you affect something it affects you back

3

You and money are in a relationship
How you relate to money will affect how it relates back to you
How you relate to money reflects how you relate to other
things

4

Your relationship to money mirrors other relationships
Your relationship with money reflects your relationship with
self
Money is a mirror

*We do not mind our not arriving anywhere nearly so much as
our not having any company on the way*
Frank Moore Colby

To love and be loved in return

Money is something we are in relationship with. Everything exists by virtue of relationship. The connection between everything is real. It is an energetic connection, which is now 'scientifically proven' in quantum physics, though it has been known by most ancient cultures for thousands of years.

If everything is connected, then this means not only that 'inanimate objects' should be regarded differently, but it also means that we can affect these objects and they can affect us back. If everything is connected, it means that the word 'relationship' can be used in relation to our car, computer, house, and also to money.

However, though we have gone into space and advanced technologically in many ways, the area of relationships is still largely uncharted terrain. We can see evidence of this all around us. So now take that fact, and add money, with all its negative clichés and parables, and all the fears and anxiety linked to it across time, and what do you get? Well, it's definitely not 'and they lived happily ever after'!

What do you say after you say hello?

Without a doubt, life and how we deal with it is best described as one long series of relationships. Yet we are never given any training in this most important area of our lives. Parents are expected to know instinctively how to relate to their children. Children are supposed to know how to relate to parents, teachers, authority, and their friends. It is assumed we know how to get on with our partners or spouses or lovers. No training is provided. No guidelines. No rules of communication, of conflict resolution, of loving. No outlines or parameters. Clearly, this method has not been providing any of the tools we need to ensure we have good relationships.

So it is no wonder that our relationship with money is often not as great as it could be. In fact our relationship with money will reflect other relationships in our life. And as we change one, so they all change. Because how you do anything is how you do everything, and because everything is connected.

This is a key concept to reflect upon, which runs as a core theme throughout this book. You will treat money in the same way as you treat others you are in relationship with. If you do not respect your partner, for example, you will not respect money, and money will respond accordingly. If you are too possessive with it, money will, eventually, leave you. If you do not love money (desire works just as well), it will not come to you, as you will not attract it.

Of course this is only one of the many aspects which influence your relationship with money. The various aspects involved in your relationship with money are interwoven and should be looked at in unison; we separate them here only for ease of reference. The key is that everything is connected and, as such, everything affects everything else.

Mirror, mirror, on the wall …

How you do anything is how you do everything. If you do not pay attention to money, you probably don't notice other things either – like the crack in the window, or your wife's new hairdo, or perhaps your aching knee. If you take pride in what you do and believe in excellence this will also be reflected in everything you do, no matter how trivial. That's just the way things are.

So money not only relates to us the way we relate to it, but it also reflects to us the way we relate to the world. Often we do not want to see this reflection, so we keep away from money. Money raises all sorts of issues for us which we would rather ignore – it questions our priorities, our ethics, our beliefs, and our trust in life. And finally it reflects to us the biggest and most important relationship of our lives – the relationship with self, because it is this, most of all, that we reflect on to our relationship with money.

If we feel we aren't deserving, if we feel we are not good enough, if we are not expressing generosity ourselves, or if we believe that we are limited in what we can do and how we can express ourselves, then these qualities will be projected on to and reflected back to us from money.

... loves me, loves me not, loves me ...

A relationship is a two-way flow of energy, it's a communication, it is an exchange. When it comes to money, it's a little like (my variation of the famous) 'ask not what money can do for you, ask rather what you can do for money'. Think about that for a while. What does money want from you?

We think of money as that thing that we need to get, or find, or win, or earn. It's there, outside, and we need to somehow 'fetch it'. Once we find it, we want to own it and get it to do what we want. Sounds a lot like some relationships, doesn't it? We do not think money should have any expectations of us. Often we do not even like it very much, or we fear it, and yet we still expect it to come to us, just because we want it to. Sometimes we are not even too sure if we do want it to come to us, but we seek it anyway.

We spend most of our lives searching for money, and then when we find it, we do not pay much attention to it. We do not care for it, or look after it. We don't even know much about what makes it tick. When it leaves us one day, we are very surprised.

Consider your relationship with money. Reflect on how you have been treating it, and ask yourself what would happen if you treated your lover or child or dog in the same way. It's quite a thought, isn't it? Also, compare how you treat money with how you treat the significant (and, more importantly, the less significant) others in your life. Also consider how others treat you.

> *There is only one journey. Going inside yourself*
> Rainer Maria Rilke

Now you may think this line of thinking is somewhat absurd, because after all what can money want from us? It's not a person, it has no needs. I remember giving a talk on money to a group of business people in Cape Town. I asked them to sit in pairs and 'talk to money'. One person would be money, and the other would simply be themselves. Each would take turns to start, and converse, allowing the discussion to emerge and flow naturally.

Some who have done this process have said that in the space of 10 to 15 minutes they learnt more about money than they had in their entire lives!

And then money said, 'Talk to me'

Anyway, a gentleman (who was in the role of 'money') was having problems with this process. He said, 'I am money. I have no emotions. I do not care. I have no feelings. Don't give me these stories about helping the poor and the orphans. I am money. I have no feelings. Why should I care?'

So I said to him in his role as 'money' and in my role as 'me', 'Well, you know you need me, money. Without me, you are nothing. You are unformed energy, you are potential, nothing more. I can help you take form. I can help you to become something.'

Now this gentleman happened to be a scholar of the classics, and immediately his face lit up. 'Oh,' he said, 'you can help me morph (this is another way of saying 'take form', which I only understood because I am Greek). I see ... Now I understand.'

Money needs us to give it form. Money needs us to turn it from an abstract nonentity into a live breathing reality. And to do that we need to enter into a relationship with it.

A relationship is a two-way process. There is a give and a take, then a take and a give. This is a continuous cycle – like we see in nature all around us. We give seeds to the earth, the earth gives us food. The rain falls into the ground and is given back into the clouds to fall again. Everything is part of a never-ending cycle. There is an apparent beginning and end, but once the cycle is in full swing it is hard to distinguish the one from the other.

The cycle is only disturbed when someone stops giving and only receives, or when someone stops receiving and just gives. Everything is connected, because everything is energy. We also know that the laws that govern nature are also the laws that govern us, as we are a part of nature. The hermetic laws say 'as above so below, as below so above'.

So therefore our relationship with money cannot be merely a process of taking. We cannot see money only as something we get. We need to also look at what we give. And, more specifically, what we give to money. What do we offer money in exchange for offering itself to us?

We have a lot to offer money, and indeed we have to offer it a lot, if we hope to attract the attention of money to us. Why should money come to me, is what you should be asking. What do you offer it? How can you help money to transform?

If you were money, where would you lodge?

Imagine for a moment that you are money. You are this enormously powerful, potent energy or force. You are powerful enough to create or destroy nations. Yet you wander aimlessly, invisible, unformed, looking for a home.

Now here is someone who wants to pay off their many bills. They are miserable, they don't like you, and they blame you for all their debt and troubles. All they want is to use you to pay off and then create more debt. That is their thinking. That is as far as their vision of money extends.

> *Without vision the people perish*
> Proverbs 29:18

Here is someone else with another vision. They want to create a future with a beautiful new house and fancy new car. They want a business in music production with studios around the world, and they also want to help feed the orphans. This person really likes you and thinks you are wonderful, and wants to care for you and look after you well and help you to grow. If you were money, where would you lodge?

The 'big, hairy, audacious goal'

(The 'big, hairy, audacious goal', fondly known as a BHAG, was first introduced to the world by James Collins and Jerry Porras.)

One of the main reasons more people are not wealthy is their lack of clear intent, and their lack of a specific greater vision. It is your intent which will capture the attention of money, acting as a magnet to harness this energy towards you. A specific and clear vision, an extraordinary dream, will enable you to contain the money.

I would like to suggest to you right now that unless you have a 'big, hairy, audacious goal', unless your future vision is slightly overwhelming in its enormity, unless you are reaching for something that is well and truly out of your present reach, not only will money not flow in huge quantities towards you, but you yourself will not be interested enough to pursue it.

We are all enormous, multitalented, beings. Beyond our personalities and egos and our 'stuff' and our excuses, each and every person has unlimited potential, because we are energy. We can literally become anything. We can create anything. One single individual has the power to enrich or destroy millions. And it is always one single individual who does just that!

> *But if you have nothing at all to create,*
> *then perhaps you create yourself'*
>
> Carl Jung

Do not hide your light under a bushel

And yet, most of us spend our lives in hiding. We act small, we deny our power and we hide our magic and our magnificence. As a result, the part of us that knows we can, the 'bigger' part of ourselves, becomes thoroughly bored. The goals we set for ourselves, mostly centred on basic survival are not appealing enough for either money or for ourselves to take an interest in.

Let's face it, are you really interested in slogging away so you can pay your bills every month? Is a 'comfortable retirement' truly what you want to set up as a goal for your life? Is that what life is all about?

Without an extraordinary dream to aspire towards, you will generate no magic, no alchemy, no energy flow. And there will be little of the magnificence of money or of yourself flowing back in consequence towards you.

But let's get back to relationships, and how you can have a good – no, let's change that to a *great* – relationship with money. It is actually a lot easier to set in motion than you may imagine. And it has little to do with working out your bank balance, or dealing with your investments or retirement plan.

First off, you must assess where your relationship with money stands at the moment. Before you can change something, you must know what it is you want to change. This means really seeing the relationship for what it is, beyond the superficialities and masks. This takes courage, non-attachment, and a sense of humour.

The following exercise will help you. Do it lightly. This is really not serious!

Using the following prompts will help to shed some light on you and your relationship with money as it stands at present. This is information which is below the tip of the iceberg. In other words, you may be surprised at what you discover, as this knowledge may not be in your conscious awareness.

Writing tips

- Keep the pen moving, don't think, just write. Allow the pen to write.
- Write for 2 minutes on each prompt. Time this.

My Relationship with Money

Wealth Training Process

1. My relationship with money is …
2. Money thinks I am …
3. If money was in an intimate relationship with me it would …

---

4. Money is similar to my partner because …

5. The recurring pattern in my relationships is …

6. I expect from a relationship that …

7. What I offer in a relationship is …

8. I expect that money should …

9. I offer money …

10. The way I can change my relationship with money is …

When you are finished, read through, highlighting anything important with a different coloured pen, or a highlighter, then summarise all of the above into one sentence.

- Assess your current position without judgement.
- Undertake to make any changes necessary.
- Record any decisions you want to make as a result of these discoveries.
- Record any actions you want to take.

Once you can look clearly at what your current relationship with money is, you can begin to change it. The key to all great relationships is attention. You need to pay attention. You must pay attention to the other party, in this case money, to yourself, and to the relationship.

A relationship is a two-way interaction. You need to decide what it is that you offer money. That will be your attention, your care, and also your extraordinary dream. Your dream will attract money to you. It will enable money to manifest itself in your life and to take form. Not only that, but extraordinary dreams usually benefit large numbers of people. This is an extra bonus, and a huge incentive for the many who want to make the world a better place.

> *Creation is only the projection into form*
> *of that which already exists*
> Shrimad Bhagavatam

To dream an extraordinary dream

To have an extraordinary dream you need first of all to believe. Believe in your ability to create magic. Believe that nothing is too good for you. Believe that you can make a difference. Believe that you are special. Believe that this is a game. Believe that it is fun. Believe that you have nothing to lose. And, above all, just believe!

You also need to be willing to expand your field of responsibility. Yes, having money is a responsibility. You need to grow up enough to become a little child to be able to handle it. Grown-up growing up is not what you want to do! That's the old, dour responsible. It's the serious, drop-dead-from-too-many-late-nights-at-the-office sort of responsible. And the wipe-that-grin-off-your-face-you're-an-adult-now;you're-not-supposed-to-be-having-fun-it's-work. That is not going to help you! Even the banks have got over being serious about money. Now their adverts show people having fun, on holiday, or helping one another.

Little children believe everything, because they simply know. Little children know they can. Little children can enter the kingdom of heaven because of this!

You don't need to suffer to prove you are a talented artist, or musician, or writer, or so much more spiritual than Those Other People with lots of money who spend their days tanning on the beach. These are old myths we still buy into subconsciously, but they are old myths, and not useful any more. Were they ever?

Changing your relationship with money

If you are still buying into such illusions, it may be time for a change. This old way of thinking is unnecessary and not doing anyone any good. It is a big mind trap, which keeps you small. You need to grow up and have some fun! You need to lighten up, so you can fly!

> *I will never go to a protest against war.*
> *But have a march for peace, and I will be there*
>
> Mother Teresa

To change your relationship with money, you need to change your relationship with money. That's not a printing error. You also need to change your relationship with yourself and with others – particularly the others that have a bearing on money. These are the 'them' whom you blame directly or indirectly for your lack of money or for their part in abusing the world's resources, or for being somehow not as good as you.

Cultivate the roses

If this blaming is your dilemma, it may be time for a change. It may be time to consider that we are all connected, and therefore we are all responsible. And therefore if we accept this, we should be asking ourselves how we can make a difference. And we should be looking to see how we could be using both our hands instead of merely the index finger.

Changing your relationship with something is a process. It is not an event. It starts with awareness. Then the willingness to change must be cultivated. Out of awareness and willingness will develop the desire for new focus. Out of new focus will arise new attention – this new attention will create new habits, and new positive actions will naturally follow. The change is a gradual process, almost imperceptible. Awareness needs daily refreshment and attention. Attention requires intention and focus. Focus needs joy and motivation. You need to be kind to yourself and start each day anew. Keep trying. It took years to cultivate your current relationships, it may take a while to readjust them towards your new aspirations.

It's like the permaculture method of gardening. You don't focus on the weeds, you focus on planting and cultivating the flowers and vegetables. The weeds are also there, in between everything, but if you don't spend your time focusing on them, they kind of wilt away. What you resist, will persist. What you focus on, expands.

Enter into the dance

Working on a relationship is an ongoing process. It is a dynamic thing, constantly being redefined. Every relationship is like a dance. Its rhythm changes throughout the song. You need to be attentive to your partner's movements, avoid standing on their toes. If you are leading, it must be so effortless that you cannot feel it. If you are following, it must be so smooth, you cannot tell. Ultimately leader and follower move as one, effortlessly.

I recommend real live dancing for many things – marketing and sales, money making, cultivating the ability to be a good negotiator or strategist, getting your timing right. The secret is to do it with attention, as a symbolic act. If you dance with the objective of using the dance as metaphor for money making, then you are performing a powerful act in the universe, which will result in a big change in the area of money, and your relationship with it; otherwise, you will simply be dancing.

When dancing in this way you will be able to see quite clearly how you relate to an 'other'. Do you simply defer? Are you easily taken off course? Do you lead? Can you follow? Are you attentive to the 'other'? Can you direct the 'other' effortlessly? How do you manoeuvre?

How well do you dance with money and with life?

My Relationship with Money, Self, and Others

Wealth Training Process

Here are some more paired questions to contemplate – gently, with kindness, and without judgement. Try to observe the patterns, if any. You may write about or merely contemplate on these. Each activity will produce different results. It is best to contemplate while in a relaxed, meditative or 'dreamy' state, while in the bath or shower, or while driving. Then you can free write.

1. How do I treat others? How do I treat money?

2. How do others treat me? How does money treat me?

3. How do I end relationships? How do my money cycles end?

4. How do I start relationships? How do I start my money cycles?

5. What makes me happy in a relationship? In relation to money?

6. What holds my relationships together? What connects me to money?

---

7. What do others reflect to me? What does money reflect to me?

8. Which aspect of myself do I like? Which aspect of money do I like?

9. Which aspect of myself do I dislike? Which aspect of money do I dislike?

10. Which aspect of others do I dislike? Which aspects of myself do others dislike? Which aspects of myself does money dislike?

11. What observations and conclusions can I draw from this?

12. What new resolutions, decisions and actions do I want to take as a result?

Everything is connected

Looking at money as something we are in relationship with changes not only how we look at money, it also changes how money looks at us. This is because everything is energy and everything is connected. Money acts as a mirror reflecting the relationships we have with others, and with self. To improve our relationship with money we need to reflect on the state of this relationship, consider the patterns in all our relationships and create the willingness for change.

It occurred to me one day that there was a pattern in my relationships which was quite different from the pattern in my best friend's relationships. I found this both strange and interesting. I noticed how in my relationships I was always the victim of infidelity, whereas in her relationships this never happened. Although she too had a definite pattern, her pattern was different from mine.

It occurred to me that this being the case, the common denominator in all my relationships was me, so perhaps this situation had something to do with me rather than the others in my life.

This was quite a revelation at nineteen, and I had planted a seed.

It took almost another decade for me to realise that the role of victim was what I resonated with, which allowed both the infidelity and the collapse of my first fortune due to debt created by my then husband. I realised that playing victim had its advantages – you are always the good guy, it's never your fault, and you always have someone to blame. Quite fabulous really, except for the heartache.

One day I said, enough. I said to myself, I will not allow you to do this to yourself any longer. And so I ended a very destructive relationship of the break-up and make-up kind with a man with a roving eye, who I was desperately and passionately in love with, and I said, no more.

And when he appeared at the door late at night, with passion in his eyes, I said to him, I may well love you forever, but I will no longer allow myself to be with you. Goodbye. Some of you will understand exactly how hard a thing this was to do.

Well, later I took another decision. I decided that I was done with infidelity, I was done with being victim, and that from that day on I would only be with men who were faithful. And do you know what? It has been so, ever since. Almost like magic. Not only that, but I also stopped being victim in my relationship with money.

Never underestimate the power of intent to change your life. And remember, everything is connected.

As we change our relationship with one thing, so will all our other relationships mirror this change. This is particularly so if we act with awareness.

To develop a good relationship with money, we need to see the relationship as a two-way interaction, looking not only at what money does for us, but also at what we can do for money. An extraordinary dream with clear intent will create a large enough container for money to flow towards, attracting money to us. Light-hearted, regular attention and communication will maintain the relationship.

Talking to Money

Wealth Training Process

How do you talk to money? Well, there are many ways to do it. You can have a two-way discussion with someone you trust, or you can do it alone, using an empty chair and taking turns to be 'you' or 'money'. You can also do some creative writing, where you use a prompt and let your hand write. Your prompt could be 'I am money, and I would like to tell you …' You can also draw an abstract drawing entitled 'what money wants to tell me' and then, looking at the drawing, free write about it.

The technique does not matter as much as your intent. Set your intent right now, to change your relationship with money to a mutually beneficial and positive one. Perform any symbolic acts to reinforce this intention. Reflect, and pay attention. Most importantly, prepare to receive.

A symbolic act is an act or ceremony which opens energetic doorways into parts of you that you may not be consciously aware of. It can open up lines of communication with dormant aspects of yourself, it may unlock energy, and it is a way to focus attention. A symbolic act sets subtle processes in motion in the energetic interconnectedness which is around you, which continue to ripple and flow and create results, in ways unimaginable to the rational mind.

Anything you do with intent and attention and some measure of reverence can become a symbolic act. For example, you may wish to take old bills and burn them on a fire, together with the intent of releasing all debt (maybe use photocopies), or you may want to buy a new wallet as a symbolic act of starting a new relationship with money. Always state the words of your intention out loud, with purpose, when you perform a symbolic act – and if you do it three times, like in the very best of tales, the outcome will be assured!

Whatever you do, have fun! Feel all the good feelings that you want money to bring, and send these to money, with love, xxxx. To expand your wallet, you must first expand your heart. Money will soon follow.

Wealth Reflections

Money as Relationship

- Everything exists by virtue of relationship
- Everything is connected, everything is energy
- Money reflects your relationship with others
- Money reflects your relationship with self
- Money is a mirror
- You are in relationship with everything
- When you change one relationship, all your relationships change
- You are in relationship with money
- Relationships are a two-way process of give and take
- Money needs you in order for it to transform
- Money needs you in order to manifest
- Money is attracted to the magical and the extraordinary
- Your extraordinary dream will attract money to you

> *Be really whole, and all things will come to you*
> Lau-Tzu

8

Money as Teacher

What is money trying to teach you?

What does money mirror to you?

Wealth Attunement

Money as Teacher

1

Money is a teacher
Money is a magnifying glass
It will mirror your darkness and your light

2

A teacher unlocks your potential
A teacher provides the soil for your growth
A teacher will help you unfold into the best you can be

3

What we are learning is who we are
What we are learning is who we can become
What we are learning is how to transcend

4

Money will teach you what is important
Money will show you the root of all evil
Money will lead you to your truth

5

When the pupil is ready the teacher appears

Learning is movement from moment to moment
J Krishnamurti

Learning to be human

What are we really trying to learn in life? What is all our education and striving and reading and enquiry all about? What is the sum total of all our experiences and all our tuition and all our learning? What do we learn, ultimately? And is it what we should be learning? Is it what we are yearning to learn?

What we really try to learn is who we are, and what is truth. We try to learn what is important, what our values are, where we draw the line as people; in effect, what it is to be human. This is what we try to learn in life. And even further than that, we try to discover the divine spark within us, the part that is beyond human.

That is what we try to learn beyond all of our learning, and we have many teachers. Teachers are all around us. Some are obvious, like our parents, actual teachers, spiritual teachers and mentors. Other teachers are not so obvious. They pose as enemies, or noisy neighbours, or our pets. It is often from these, the less obvious teachers, that we learn our most valuable lessons. And I believe one of the greatest of these less obvious teachers is money.

Imagine for a moment that you wanted to place a teacher on this planet that could be all things to all people. A teacher that could direct the course of your life, but in a very subtle and imperceptible way. Imagine you wanted to hide the existence of this teacher, so no one would know that she was there. (Of course she's a woman.) Imagine that you wanted to make sure that everyone not only learnt their lessons, but that the lessons expanded as the student grew. What could you do?

> *Everyone is ignorant, only in different subjects*
> Will Roger

Well, you could create a teacher called money. A teacher that is invisible but appears to be visible. An interactive teacher that is both teacher and lesson. She can take the form of anything depending on a person's consciousness and intent. She can lead the way or block the way, but certainly she will direct the way of everyone in her path. She will appear as one thing, yet be another – an undercover operator. She will be everywhere and nowhere all at the same time. She will be closely linked with every person and their lives from birth to death.

A teacher called money.

Consider that.

Rich Man, Poor Man, Rich Man – A Romanian Tale

I am a storyteller, as was my father before me, and it was through some of these tales that I learnt many of my lessons. My father was born in Romania, the eldest son of a Greek father and a Romanian mother. There were six children in the family and, although not wealthy, they lived comfortably in the rural town of Braila in a rambling house surrounded by cherry trees.

When the communists took over in Romania, there was a change of currency. It was announced that at noon on a certain day 'old' Lei would be scrapped and 'new' Lei would be issued. Everyone could legally exchange however much old currency they had for the new currency up to a certain maximum amount which was equal for all. Any surplus old currency would thereafter have no value. And each citizen would now own no more than the maximum, permitted amount of the new currency.

Of course there were those in power, those holding high ranking positions in the army, and the extremely wealthy who were subject to different rules and, as a result, fortunes were created in a short, but roaring, black market trade.

Imagine for a moment that you have, say, $100 000 of old currency in your bank account, which you are allowed to exchange for $10 000 of the new currency. The rest you simply have to throw away. However, you know of someone who is willing to exchange the balance of $90 000 for a third of its value.

That's the position my father was in as he headed for the station with a suitcase full of cash at dawn on that last day, on his way to meet a certain captain in another town. Unfortunately, he was too late. The captain had bought up all the money he could, and there was nothing more to be done.

> *The only person who is educated is the one*
> *who has learned how to learn ... and change*
>
> Carl Rogers

The money, my friend, is blowing in the wind

The story goes that as the train pulled into the station on my father's return, the clock struck midday. My father disembarked, placed the suitcase filled with money on the platform, opened it, and walked away as the notes blew away in the wind.

It is a powerful picture, regardless of the actual facts, and it has a special place in my memories, as I know it did in my father's. It was one of my earliest lessons in money. That it is transient, that you cannot depend on its existence for wealth, that it can lose or gain value overnight.

Yet even though one of my father's favourite sayings, distilled no doubt from this experience, was 'everything passes, my child, everything passes', what I learnt from this story is that we endure.

He walked away from the money blowing in the wind, and he endured. I, too, have done this metaphorically several times in my life, for various reasons. Money will come and go in your life, but only you will endure. Therefore you are more powerful than money. In fact, you are the source of the money. You are the one who creates the money. You are the money. That is one of the first lessons I learnt about money – that the money comes from me.

There is no security in life, only opportunity
Mark Twain

What is at the end of the tale?

I did not know I had learnt this lesson until later. In fact, since becoming a parent I have come to really understand how deeply and profoundly we imprint our children with our attitudes and beliefs without saying a single word. In the course of writing and presenting courses on the subject of money, and in thinking back on my own life, I have become aware that many of my beliefs have been shaped by my parents. Not so much by anything they said or did, but by their underlying attitudes that emanated non-verbally, and also by my personal distillation and understanding of the things they told me. Then, as I went through life, I built upon these lessons and learnt new ones too.

It is important to know what lessons you have learnt, especially with regard to money, as it will affect the way you attract money flow into your life. Sometimes we think we have learnt one lesson, when in fact it was another. Here is an opportunity to examine the lessons that money has taught you in life, with an opportunity to reconfigure the moral of the story where necessary. This requires that you cast a different point of view over your life. We'll do that now.

Take a few moments to relax and loosen your mind. Take a few deep breaths. Perhaps shake out your arms and shoulders.

Imagine that your mind is relaxing also, it is becoming loose and liquid, not holding on to anything too strongly. Now in this relaxed, contemplative state, gently drop a question into your mind.

What Lessons have I Learnt about Money?

Wealth Training Process

Ask yourself: What lessons have I learnt about money? Then list each idea and thought as it arises. List every cliché and parable, as it arises. Number your list, and go to number 20. Do not censor anything. Simply write. If you become lost, repeat the prompt to yourself.

When you are finished, read through and think of where each lesson came from. Who told you this? Was it your mother, a friend, did you read it in a book, was it the result of a personal experience? Write the source of each lesson next to each point. When you are finished, highlight anything important with a different coloured pen, or a highlighter. Assess your current position without judgement.

- Undertake to make any changes necessary.
- Record any decisions you want to make as a result of these discoveries.
- Record any actions you want to take.

Without a doubt, some of your money lessons will be conclusions or 'morals of the story' drawn at a time of your life when you felt differently from how you feel now. If your conclusions today are different, or if some of these lessons are no longer relevant, cross out the old, and rewrite, drawing a new conclusion. It is important to physically cross out the outdated beliefs, as this makes an impact on the mind. Draw a new conclusion. And then draw 'a new conclusion' for good measure.

Excuse me?

Drawing New Conclusions about Money

Wealth Training Process

Take a large piece of paper and write 'Drawing New Conclusions about Money' as a heading. Then, using your crayons, draw whatever arises. Allow what emerges to emerge. When you are finished, allow your pen to write, using the drawing as a prompt. What you write will surprise you.

If you are used to this method of working, then you need no convincing that it is profound beyond measure. If, on the other hand, you have never written, or 'drawn conclusions', it is best that you don't until you do … Allow yourself to be amazed at how something that sounds so simple, even trite, can produce such amazing events.

This is the beginning of the journey. Be interested to see how it unfolds!

To teach what you most need to learn

So if money is your teacher, what could it be teaching you? Well, it is different for everyone, but it is very much a composite of everything else you have read about in this book about mirror, and shadow, and transformation, and relationship all being an expression of energy which, through the process of alchemy, is being transformed into a new you.

Money is teaching all of us about energy, about intransience, about the illusionary nature of materialism, about transcending duality, and if all that sounds too esoteric, let me put it another way. Money is teaching us that things are not always the way they seem. Money is teaching us that everything is energy, and that you can create and direct with this energy. And money uses itself to illustrate this lesson.

Money teaches us that in the end, it's all about us. We are what we are creating, we are what we are transforming, we are what we are growing. It is all about us. Money will reflect to us how we see ourselves, and how we project our shadow into the outside world through our view of money. When we project lack, we receive lack. When we project meanness, we receive meanness. When we project generosity, we receive generosity. When we project abundance, we receive abundance.

Look around you closely. Look around at yourself. Observe how you relate in relation to money and in relation to money and others. Observe your internal dialogue when it is time to pay the bill, for example. Do you think people or the world 'owes you'? Are you a taker or a giver?

To love and be loved in return

This is quite a big topic. We all like to think we are givers. Similarly, some of us are unable to receive. The universe is actually constantly trying to assist us, people around us are trying to assist us, but often we do not know how to receive. Receiving is very closely linked to giving. In fact, if we are unable to receive, we are actually not fully able to give, and vice versa. Everything is linked.

To receive, to embrace the world and its gifts, means to open our arms. This means we need to open our hearts. This is scary. With open arms we are exposed, we are open, we are vulnerable. Simply admitting we need help is often difficult. Yet we cannot receive help unless we do this.

> *'What makes the desert beautiful,' said the little prince, 'is that somewhere it hides a well ...'*
>
> from *The Little Prince by* Antoine De Saint-Exupéry

Seven money making pathways

The lessons that money teaches are many. I will touch on some of the more obvious ones, and invite you to contemplate your own life from these perspectives. These topics are presented as a series of questions for reflection. They are all powerful pathways that will lead you to wealth.

1. **The cycle of give and receive**

2. **Respect others as you do yourself – Respect other things as you do others**

3. **Attention**

4. **Openness and Generosity**

5. **Expansion and Containment**

6. **Simplicity**

7. **Trust**

You can reflect upon, free write about, or draw around these topics and the related questions that follow. Before you start, state your intent, which can be something along the lines of: 'Through these reflections, I intend to discover and transform aspects of myself and my relationship with money for the

---

purpose of expanding my wealth, in terms of the highest good for all.'

When you are finished with each section, highlight or underline anything important with a different coloured pen, or a highlighter. Assess your current position without judgement. Keep it light and fun. Make it an exploration. Be curious!

1. The Cycle of Give and Receive

Wealth Training Process

You receive in direct relation, not only to the quantity, but also to the quality of your giving.

1. What do I give? Where do I give? How do I give?
2. What do I hold back? Why?
3. How do I refuse to give?
4. What do I receive? Where do I receive? How do I receive?
5. How do I refuse to receive?
6. Where does the give and receive cycle in my life get stuck?
7. Where can I give, to benefit others, without reward?
8. What can I give to money? How can I give to money?
9. What can I give to myself? How can I prepare to receive?
10. What does money teach me about giving and receiving?

- Record any decisions made as a result of these discoveries.
- Undertake to make any changes necessary.
- Write down any actions you want to take.Keep it light!

The beginning is the most important part of the work

Plato

Open your arms wide

You give only as much as you are able to receive. If you imagine yourself as a jug, you can easily understand this. The jug will only pour out as much as is in there. And yet, paradoxically, to increase your ability to receive, you must increase your ability to give. You need to plant seeds before you can harvest the crop. To increase your ability to receive, you must open up your arms and let go of whatever you are clutching to your chest. (It does not matter why you are clutching it – just let it go – this is a decision you can make right now, if you want to.) This is an act of faith and trust.

After my experience in my first business, I could have closed myself off to future possibilities. I could have said 'no' to my new business partner. I could have decided not to trust him, or life, or myself. I could have decided not to go into business again. I could have listened to my father and got myself a decent job or finished my university studies. Instead, I opened my arms wide to receive bigger and better things.

Giving has always been a big part of my daily practice, since a very young age. I never stopped this, even when I had little to give. When I really had very little, I would leave my old red Ford Capri car unlocked with a blanket on the back seat for a certain homeless person to sleep in at night. I would drop off my leftovers each morning with a (very grumpy) man who always scowled at me in the alleyway next to my block of flats.

These were very small things that I did, but I believe they kept my money flow open and, more importantly, they kept my heart open to receive.

You cannot receive with your arms closed. The door will not open until you knock. You will not find until you seek. You hold the key. You are the start of the give and take cycle. You start by giving.

---

2. Respect others as you do yourself – Respect other things as you do others

Wealth Training Process

How you respect money and possessions is directly related to the energy and love you have poured into their creation.

1. What do I respect? Who do I respect? How do I respect?
2. Who respects me?
3. How do I respect myself?
4. What do I respect about money?
5. How do I show money my respect?
6. What do I respect about those who have mastered money making?
7. How do I respect my possessions?
8. How do I respect my talents and gifts?
9. How do I respect the gift of life?
10. What does money teach me about respect?

- Record any decisions made as a result of these discoveries.
- Undertake to make any changes necessary.
- Write down any actions you want to take. Keep it light!

He has so much money, he'll never miss it …

A man looks out across a field of lavender stretching as far as the eye can see. He admires the lavender. He may even envy the farmer who has grown so much lavender. He may think the farmer does not know how much lavender he has, because the field is so big. He may think the farmer will not miss a bunch here and there if it went missing, because he has so much.

The farmer looks across the field of lavender he has grown. He thinks back to the day when the field was nothing more than arid soil and rock. He remembers the digging and the ploughing, and the fertilising. He remembers the planting, and the tending of each little seedling, protecting it from hail and pest and drought. He has walked this field in every weather, up and down through the rows of plants. He knows each corner intimately, he jokes that he may even know each plant by name.

How you respect money and possessions is directly related to the energy and love you have poured into their creation. It has nothing to do with how materialistic you perceive yourself to be.

Everything is energy. Everything is linked. Your respect of something, whether it is a person, money, or a tree, reflects your respect of self and your recognition of the divinity which resides within every part of creation. And as you recognise this divinity, so it resonates back to you, mirroring your own wondrousness and expanding it. This is in fact how money really grows. This is money alchemy.

There is a story of the Indian monk who had to walk through the forest each day. And each day as he walked he would greet the divinity within each animal, and as a result none of the animals harmed him, not even the tigers.

I, too, have found this to be true. I have been in many tricky situations in my life, I have been in many 'wrong' places, sometimes with the 'wrong' people. I have been in grave danger, and the only thing that has kept me safe is the belief that within each and every one of us there lies a divine spark, waiting to be ignited. I believe in addressing the best in others, acknowledging and appealing to the highest within them.

When you do this, when you respect the oneness that links us all together, then you echo the words of an Indian Elder that go:

> *I honour that place in you where the Universe resides*
> *And when you are in that place in you,*
> *and I am in that place in me,*
> *Then there is only one of us.*

That, too, is alchemy.

---

3. Attention

Wealth Training Process

To make money you must put your attention on making money.

1. Where do I put my attention each day?
2. What am I not paying attention to each day?
3. How much attention goes into my needs/desires/passions?
4. How do I pay attention to my body/ emotions/thoughts/spirit?
5. How much attention do I give to my loved ones?
6. How do I pay attention to money?
7. What is money drawing my attention to?
8. What do I need to put my attention on?
9. What do I need to release from my attention?
10. What does money teach me about attention?

- Record any decisions made as a result of these discoveries.
- Undertake to make any changes necessary.
- Write down any actions you want to take. Keep it light!

Pay attention. Be here, now. Pay attention. Look. Listen. Observe. Be. Without attention nothing can be accomplished. What you focus on expands. The power of your attention is like the power of faith – with something the size of a mustard seed, you can move mountains.

---

4. Openness and Generosity

Wealth Training Process

Until we make room for money in our lives, it cannot come to stay.

1. How open am I to receiving?
2. Where do I express generosity in my life?
3. How do loved ones express generosity towards me?
4. How do strangers express generosity towards me?
5. How do I express generosity to loved ones?
6. How do I express generosity to strangers?
7. How can I open my heart to generosity?
8. Where can I show my openness and generosity?
9. How has money been generous to me?
10. What does money teach me about openness and generosity?

- Record any decisions made as a result of these discoveries.
- Undertake to make any changes necessary.
- Write down any actions you want to take. Keep it light!

If you follow your bliss, you will put yourself on a kind of track, which has been there all the while waiting for you, and the life you ought to be living will be the one you are living.

Joseph Campbell

Preparing to receive

For money to flow towards us, we need to be open. This is an attitude to cultivate. It is a frame of mind which is yielding, accepting, grateful, thankful, celebratory, prepared and ready to receive. Unless we open the door, money cannot enter. Until we make room for money in our lives, it cannot come to stay. We need to prepare the feast and make ready to receive with joy.

The practice of generosity is a wonderful means of keeping your channels of flow open and preparing you to receive. Generosity tunes you in to the frequency of prosperity and abundance. It creates magnificently positive ripples to flow all around you attracting all good things.

The practice of generosity does not depend on money. You can be generous with your time, your affection, your attention, your energy, your compliments, your smile. You can be generous with your patience, your reverence, your understanding, and your humour. And as you give generously, so it will be generously given to you. That is universal law.

---

5. Expansion and Containment

Wealth Training Process

To create wealth you need to contain more.

1. What needs to expand in my life?
2. Which area of my life needs to grow to contain money?
3. What beliefs need to expand to accommodate a wealthy me?
4. Which attitudes need to grow to tolerate more money?

---

5. When will I be able to contain more?
6. What can I do to expand my ability to contain?
7. How can I practise having more?
8. What do I need to let go of, to make space in my container?
9. Who can help me to expand?
10. What does money teach me about expansion and containment?

- Record any decisions made as a result of these discoveries.
- Undertake to make any changes necessary.
- Write down any actions you want to take. Keep it light!

To contain more, you must become more

To become wealthy, you need to expand, become more of who you truly are. You must expand your beliefs, your attitudes, your emotions, your wishes, your goals, your expectations. You must break out of your current comfort zone, smash through the ceiling as you now see it. Believe the unimaginable, strive towards the unthinkable.

To create wealth you need to contain more. To contain more you must increase your container, your ability to have, your ability to be. To contain more you must become more. You are already more than you are, you need to contain that!

6. Simplicity

Wealth Training Process

Money can complicate or simplify your life, depending on what you want and what you choose.

1. What are the simple facts of my needs?
2. Simply put, what do I really want?
3. Where can I simplify my life?
4. What do I need to do to simplify my life?
5. What do I need to let go of to simplify my life?
6. Where can I live a simple life?
7. What does simplicity mean to me?
8. What is really stopping me?
9. What do I need, to create simplicity and ease?
10. What does money teach me about simplicity?

- Record any decisions made as a result of these discoveries.
- Undertake to make any changes necessary.
- Write down any actions you want to take. Keep it light!

Keeping life simple is a gift. Creating simplicity, ease, grace in what we do and how we live life is a real blessing. Find out what you really want. Know what it really is that you need to keep you contented and happy. Don't spend your life accumulating, if this is not what you want or need. Find out what you need. Know what you want. Keep it simple. This means something different for everyone.

7. Trust

Wealth Training Process

Without trust nothing is possible. You need to trust. There are no guarantees, only trust.

1. Who do I trust? What do I trust? How do I trust? What does trust mean to me?
2. Who trusts me?
3. What do I trust about money?
4. What do I trust about myself?
5. What do I trust about life?
6. Where do I put my trust?
7. How do I contain trust?
8. What can I do to develop my trust?
9. What do I need to cultivate trust?
10. What does money teach me about trust?

- Record any decisions made as a result of these discoveries.
- Undertake to make any changes necessary.
- Write down any actions you want to take. Keep it light!

If you can trust yourself, you can trust others

Without trust nothing is possible. You need to trust yourself first, before you can trust anyone else. You need to trust that you know, that you can, that you will, that you are able, that you can overcome, that you can create, that you can be, that you are. You need to believe, to have faith. That is all trust.

> *Trust in God, but tie your camel first*
> Old Proverb

If you can trust yourself, you can trust life, you can trust the process, you can trust the universe to deliver, you can trust money to come to you, you can trust your intuition. You need to trust. There are no guarantees, only trust.

For more than ten years I was in partnership in my portfolio management company with a wonderful man. We shared everything straight down the line. We trusted each other totally. We started, grew, ran, and sold a very profitable fund management business. We have also been involved in other businesses as investors, directors, shareholders. Our business dealings together now span eighteen years. Yet we have never had a written agreement between us. Only trust.

It has been said that if you can trust your partners you don't need an agreement, but if you cannot trust your partners, no agreement will help you.

This is not a course of action for everyone, and I would not go as far as to outrage all the business people reading this book by suggesting 'no written agreements' as a business strategy. In fact many of the people I have coached in the past will attest to my insistence on having proper business agreements in place!

I speak here only of what has worked for me. I know such partnerships are rare. But if we can leave the doors of possibility open to trust, then nothing is impossible.

> *Freedom consists not in refusing to recognise anything above*
> *us, but in respecting something which is above us;*
> *for by respecting it, we raise ourselves to it,*
> *and by our very acknowledgement,*
> *prove that we bear within ourselves what is higher,*
> *and are worthy to be on a level with it*
>
> Goethe

Wealth Reflections

Money as Teacher

- Money is a teacher
- Money teaches what you most need to learn
- Money's lessons are many, amongst them:
    - Generosity and Openness
    - Cycle of Give and Receive
    - Attention
    - Trust
    - Expansion and Containment
    - Respect
    - Simplicity
- Money will reveal your lead so you can transform it to gold
- Money will mirror your expectations and resonance
- Money can guide you to your highest potential
- Through money you can discover the teacher within

9

The
Complete Money
Alchemy Wealth Training
Processes

Just remain in the centre, watching.
Then forget that you are there

Lau-tzu

Tools you will need for processing

The processing requires the following tools:

- A large A4 Wealth Journey book that you can write in
- A pen
- Several pieces of large, blank, poster cardboard paper – A3 – white is best
- A box of nice crayons, pastels, coloured felt tip pens or coloured pencils, or the whole lot
- An egg timer, or other type of timing device
- No logic
- No seriousness
- No correction
- No censoring
- No one to ever look at what you have done, ever (unless you want it)
- An open mind

Give yourself time and space to do this work. Be aware that you may feel very tired after some of the processes. Take time to rest. Take time to integrate the shifts and changes.

REMEMBER: There is no wrong way to do any of the processes in this book.

Imagination

Connecting with I Can (or How to Imagine)

Set aside 15 minutes to dream and imagine.
- Sit in a quiet room in a comfortable chair where you will be undisturbed for about 15 minutes
- Breathe in deeply to the count of 3, hold for 3 and breathe out for 3 – or use a count of 4 or 5

- Continue to breathe rhythmically for a few minutes (using any comfortable count) until your body and mind have settled
- Now relax each part of your body in turn, slowly from head to toe, by putting your attention on it, and saying 'relax', until you are totally relaxed and calm
- Think back to a time or moment when life felt fresh and new and full of potential
- Think back to a time when you could let your imagination roam free, when you knew you could do anything
- Think back to a time when you believed
- (Each prompt could be a separate event or the same one)
- Enter that moment fully, reliving all sights and sounds, tastes, and sensations
- Feel how you felt, and feel that feeling now, expanding through your body
- Locate the part of your body where the feeling appears to originate
- Practise moving your attention to that part of the body and then moving away
- Practise turning on that feeling of *I Can*, of expansion, of yes-ness – keep connected to the feeling for as long as you can
- Return to the present when you are ready
- Ensure you are in the present. Say 'It is (date) and I am here in (place, city, country). Then touch the ground and all four walls around you, repeating the above. This is very important – do not miss this step!!

The more you practise this exercise, the more proficient you will become at it.

Everything arises from this simple task. Anything you want to create, including wealth, depends on your ability to find this channel on your dial. Once you are able to make this connection at will, practise each morning in your bath or shower. It will reap enormous benefits.

Writing tips

- Keep the pen moving, don't think, just write. Allow the pen to write.
- Write for 2 minutes on each prompt. Time this.

Money

These processes will give you a deeper understanding of you and your relationship with money. Each time you write, the data you uncover will be different. Give yourself permission to discover things about yourself you never knew before. Allow what emerges to appear without censorship.

Discovering Money

1. Money is ...
2. The truth about money is ...
3. What I like about money is ...
4. What I dislike about money is ...
5. I fear money, because ...
6. When I think about money I feel ...
7. The colour/taste/smell/texture/sound/shape of money is ... (do each one separately)
8. What money thinks of me is ...

9. If money was a person, it would be …

When you are finished, read through, highlighting anything important with a different coloured pen, or a highlighter, then summarise all of the above into one sentence.

Viewing money with the right brain

a) Using a large piece of paper and coloured crayons of your choice, draw money. Yes, that is not a misprint, 'Draw money'. What does that mean? Just see what emerges. Draw for about 5 minutes.

b) Then, while looking at your drawing, write about it.

c) Turn the drawing upside down and write about that.

d) Highlight the important bits, then summarise into one sentence.

Writing the money tale

a) Write your money autobiography, for 5 minutes.

b) You can write it in the first or third person (as I or s/he).

c) You can write it as a fairy tale or story beginning with 'once upon a time …'

d) Highlight the important bits, then summarise into one sentence.

Money beliefs, quotes and anecdotes

a) Write a numbered list of your money beliefs. Write for 5 minutes.

b) Read through, and mark the origin of each belief. Where did it come from? For example, mother/priest/girlfriend/incident with cookie jar

c) Highlight the important bits, then summarise into one sentence.

Money, money, money

Write for 2 minutes on each prompt.

a) What I know about money is …

b) What I don't know about money is …

c) I am like money because …

d) Money came to me on a sultry, moonlit night, and …

e) Later, I saw the darker side of money …

Highlight the important bits, then summarise into one sentence.

Summarise all the above sections into one sentence.

Self and Wealth

Finding your elusive self

1. I am …
2. I am not …
3. I am at a place in my life which is …
4. I am at a time in my life which is …

5. I am here because …
6. I would leave this place if …
7. The colour/taste/smell/texture/sound/shape of 'me here' is … (do each one for 2 minutes)
8. I got to this place in my life through …
9. I would not be here if …

When you are finished, read through, highlighting anything important with a different coloured pen or a highlighter, then summarise all of the above into one sentence. Do not analyse, ponder on, or become attached to what has emerged. Simply observe. Trust the process.

Looking in on your ideal future

This exercise is very useful. You can write it out, or do it in your mind's eye in daydream mode while sitting relaxed in a chair, or lying down on your bed. Doing both forms is best. This is an ongoing project, so you can keep working on it and refining it during those dull moments in traffic, in the shower, or during boring meetings. The more detail and emotion you can infuse into the picture the better.

• Imagine a day living your ideal future. Imagine yourself waking up in your bed. Look at the bedroom and describe it. Look at who is there with you. Get up and look in the mirror, see the face looking back at you and observe everything about it, including the way it feels, the energy it radiates. Look at what happens next. Notice your surroundings in as much detail as possible. See your day unfold slowly around you, as you watch. See, feel, and imagine.

- Repeat as often as you like, adjusting and refining details each time.

- Become familiar with, and embrace this you from the future.

- Get to know the hopes and aspirations of your future self.

- Allow the future to unfold.

What it means to be wealthy

Being Wealthy

1. Being wealthy means ...
2. To be really wealthy I would have to be ...
3. If I had lots of money I would need to become ...
4. If I had lots of money I would need to change ...
5. If I had lots of money I could no longer be ...
6. If I was truly wealthy I could ...
7. The person who would most dislike my being wealthy is ..., because ...
8. When I am very wealthy I will get rid of ...
9. Before I can become wealthy, I need to let go of ...

When finished, highlight anything important and then summarise into one sentence.

The Wealthy

1. The wealthiest person I know is …
2. S/he … is … because …
3. I think the very wealthy are …
4. To become extremely wealthy you need to …
5. You definitely cannot become very wealthy without …
6. When you are very wealthy, you have to …
7. What I dislike about the wealthy is …
8. What I envy about the very wealthy is …
9. List all the clichés, beliefs, and parables you have heard about wealth and the wealthy
10. Mark next to each one, its source – where did you first hear/decide this?

When finished, highlight anything important and then summarise into one sentence.

Containing Money

What do you contain?

The following exercises will help you to focus on the metaphor of container from many different angles. Allow yourself to learn about yourself. Permit yourself to reveal layers below the surface. Know that this new knowledge is yours to keep. You need not share it with anyone. No one is watching you write. No one will read what you write. Let rip!

Drawing my container

- Set aside 10 minutes for this exercise
- Get a large sheet of blank paper (A4 or bigger) and a box of crayons
- Label the paper 'my container'
- For 3 minutes draw your container – don't think about this
- Then, looking at your drawing, write about it for 5 minutes
- Underline important words or phrases and summarise into a sentence
- Turn the picture upside down
- Write about what you see now – don't think about it
- Underline important words or phrases and summarise into a sentence
- Observe your container and, without judgement, see:
    – whether it is big or small

    – tall or short

    – what it is made of

    – are the walls thick or thin?

    – does it have a firm base, is it supported?

    – is there a base at all?

    – is the opening at the top wide or narrow?

    – does it leak?

Underline important words or phrases and summarise into a sentence.

Containing my world

Using the prompts below, write for 2 minutes on each of the following: (Keep your hand moving, repeat the prompt if you get stuck)

- I contain .....
  I do not contain .....
- My body contains .....
  My body does not contain .....
- My beliefs contain ....
  My beliefs do not contain .....
- My thinking contains .....
  My thinking does not contain .....
- My talents contain .....
  My talents do not contain .....
- My skills contain .....
  My skills do not contain .....
- My views contain .....
  My views do not contain .....
- My heart contains .....
  My heart does not contain .....
- My dreams contain .....
  My dreams do not contain .....
- My goals contain .....
  My goals do not contain .....
- My money contains .....
  My money does not contain .....
- My vision contains .....
  My vision does not contain .....
- My life contains .....
  My life does not contain .....
- My potential contains .....
  My potential does not contain .....

Underline important words or phrases and summarise into a sentence.

How my world contains me

Repeat all the above prompts, switched around to read:

- I contain my body.
  I do not contain my body
- I contain my beliefs
  I do not contain my beliefs and so on
- Underline important words or phrases and summarise into a sentence.

Summarise the entire exercise into one sentence.

Containing magic

Write about, reflect upon, contemplate the following:

- If you had all the money in the world, what would you like to do?
- And then what would you have? (continue asking this 7x)
- What is your earliest memory of your ideal future/ profession?
- What do you really, really want to do, really?
- If you had a container, what would it be?
- What would you have inside and outside your container?
- What is your container made of?
- What is your potential? How do you contain it?
- What is your dream? How do you contain it?
- Make a wish list of everything you want. Be specific. Don't be shy.
- What do you really want?

Money and Relationships

My relationship with money

1. My relationship with money is …
2. Money thinks I am …
3. If money was in an intimate relationship with me it would …
4. Money is similar to my partner because …
5. The recurring pattern in my relationships is …
6. I expect from a relationship that …
7. What I offer in a relationship is …
8. I expect that money should …
9. I offer money …
10. The way I can change my relationship with money is …

When you are finished, read through, highlighting anything important with a different coloured pen, or a highlighter, then summarise all of the above into one sentence. .

My relationship with money, self, and others

Here are some more paired questions to contemplate – gently, with kindness, and without judgement. Try to observe the patterns, if any. You may write about or merely contemplate these. Each activity will produce different results. It is best to contemplate while in a relaxed, meditative or 'dreamy' state, while in the bath or shower, or while driving. Then you can free write.

1. How do I treat others? How do I treat money?

2. How do others treat me? How does money treat me?

3. How do I end relationships? How do my money cycles end?

4. How do I start relationships? How do I start my money cycles?

5. What makes me happy in a relationship? In relation to money?

6. What holds my relationships together? What connects me to money?

7. What do others reflect to me? What does money reflect to me?

8. Which aspect of myself do I like? Which aspect of money do I like?

9. Which aspect of myself do I dislike? Which aspect of money do I dislike?

10. Which aspect of others do I dislike? Which aspects of myself do others dislike? Which aspects of myself does money dislike?

11. What observations and conclusions can I draw from this?

12. What new resolutions, decisions and actions do I want to take as a result?

Talking to money

How do you talk to money? Well, there are many ways to do it. You can have a two-way discussion with someone you trust, or you can do it alone, using an empty chair and taking turns to be 'you' or 'money'. You can also do some creative writing, where you use a prompt and let your hand write. Your prompt could be 'I am money, and I would like to tell you ...' You can also draw an abstract drawing entitled 'what money wants to tell me' and then, looking at the drawing, free write about it.

The technique does not matter as much as your intent. Set your intent right now, to change your relationship with money to a mutually beneficial and positive one. Perform any symbolic acts to reinforce this intention. Reflect, and pay attention. Most importantly, prepare to receive.

Money Making Alchemy Pathways

What lessons have I learnt about money?

Ask yourself: What lessons have I learnt about money? Then list each idea and thought as it arises. List every cliché and parable, as it arises. Number your list, and go to number 20. Do not censor anything. Simply write. If you become lost, repeat the prompt to yourself.

When you are finished, read through and think of where each lesson came from. Who told you this? Was it your mother, a friend, did you read it in a book, was it the result of a personal experience? Write the source of each lesson next to each point. When you are finished, highlight anything important with a different coloured pen, or a highlighter. Assess your current position without judgement.

- Undertake to make any changes necessary.
- Record any decisions you want to make as a result of these discoveries.
- Record any actions you want to take

Without a doubt, some of your money lessons will be conclusions or 'morals of the story' drawn at a time of your life when you felt differently from how you feel now. If your conclusions today are different, or if some of these lessons are no longer relevant, cross out the old, and rewrite, drawing a new conclusion. It is important to physically cross out the outdated beliefs, as this makes an impact on the mind. Draw a new conclusion. And then draw 'a new conclusion' for good measure.

Excuse me?

Drawing new conclusions about money

Take a large piece of paper and write 'Drawing New Conclusions about Money' as a heading. Then, using your crayons, draw whatever arises. Allow what emerges to emerge. When you are finished, allow your pen to write, using the drawing as a prompt. What you write will surprise you.

Seven Money Making Alchemy Pathways

1. The cycle of give and receive
2. Respect others as you do yourself – Respect other things as you do others
3. Attention
4. Openness and Generosity
5. Expansion and Containment
6. Simplicity
7. Trust

1. The cycle of give and receive

You receive in direct relation, not only to the quantity, but also to the quality of your giving.

1. What do I give? Where do I give? How do I give?
2. What do I hold back? Why?
3. How do I refuse to give?
4. What do I receive? Where do I receive? How do I receive?
5. How do I refuse to receive?
6. Where does the give and receive cycle in my life get stuck?
7. Where can I give, to benefit others, without reward?
8. What can I give to money? How can I give to money?
9. What can I give to myself? How can I prepare to receive?
10. What does money teach me about giving and receiving?

- Record any decisions made as a result of these discoveries.
- Undertake to make any changes necessary.
- Write down any actions you want to take.   Keep it light!

2. Respect others as you do yourself – Respect other things as you do others

How you respect money and possessions is directly related to the energy and love you have poured into their creation.

1. What do I respect? Who do I respect? How do I respect?
2. Who respects me?
3. How do I respect myself?
4. What do I respect about money?
5. How do I show money my respect?
6. What do I respect about those who have mastered money making?
7. How do I respect my possessions?
8. How do I respect my talents and gifts?
9. How do I respect the gift of life?
10. What does money teach me about respect?

- Record any decisions made as a result of these discoveries.
- Undertake to make any changes necessary.
- Write down any actions you want to take. Keep it light!

3. Attention

To make money you must put your attention on making money.

1. Where do I put my attention each day?
2. What am I not paying attention to each day?
3. How much attention goes into my needs/desires/passions?
4. How do I pay attention to my body/emotions/thoughts/spirit?
5. How much attention do I give to my loved ones?
6. How do I pay attention to money?
7. What is money drawing my attention to?!

8. What do I need to put my attention on?

9. What do I need to release from my attention?

10. What does money teach me about attention?

- Record any decisions made as a result of these discoveries.
- Undertake to make any changes necessary.
- Write down any actions you want to take. Keep it light!

4. Openness and Generosity

Until we make room for money in our lives, it cannot come to stay.

1. How open am I to receiving?

2. Where do I express generosity in my life?

3. How do loved ones express generosity towards me?

4. How do strangers express generosity towards me?

5. How do I express generosity to loved ones?

6. How do I express generosity to strangers?

7. How can I open my heart to generosity?

8. Where can I show my openness and generosity?

9. How has money been generous to me?

10. What does money teach me about openness and generosity?

- Record any decisions made as a result of these discoveries.
- Undertake to make any changes necessary.
- Write down any actions you want to take. Keep it light!

5. Expansion and Containment

To create wealth you need to contain more.

1. What needs to expand in my life?
2. Which area of my life needs to grow to contain money?
3. What beliefs need to expand to accommodate a wealthy me?
4. Which attitudes need to grow to tolerate more money?
5. When will I be able to contain more?
6. What can I do to expand my ability to contain?
7. How can I practise having more?
8. What do I need to let go of, to make space in my container?
9. Who can help me to expand?
10. What does money teach me about expansion and containment?

- Record any decisions made as a result of these discoveries.
- Undertake to make any changes necessary.
- Write down any actions you want to take. Keep it light!

6. Simplicity

Money can complicate or simplify your life, depending on what you want and what you choose.

1. What are the simple facts of my needs?
2. Simply put, what do I really want?
3. Where can I simplify my life?
4. What do I need to do to simplify my life?

5. What do I need to let go of to simplify my life?
6. Where can I live a simple life?
7. What does simplicity mean to me?
8. What is really stopping me?
9. What do I need, to create simplicity and ease?
10. What does money teach me about simplicity?

- Record any decisions made as a result of these discoveries.
- Undertake to make any changes necessary.
- Write down any actions you want to take. Keep it light!

7. *Trust*

Without trust nothing is possible. You need to trust. There are no guarantees, only trust.

1. Who do I trust? What do I trust? How do I trust? What does trust mean to me?
2. Who trusts me?
3. What do I trust about money?
4. What do I trust about myself?
5. What do I trust about life?
6. Where do I put my trust?
7. How do I contain trust?
8. What can I do to develop my trust?
9. What do I need to cultivate trust?
10. What does money teach me about trust?

- Record any decisions made as a result of these discoveries.
- Undertake to make any changes necessary.
- Write down any actions you want to take. Keep it light!

10

Money Alchemy - Wealth Reflections

Creating Money Alchemy

- Alchemy is about transformation

- Making money is a process of transformation

- Money alchemy can transform your physical reality

- Money alchemy can transform you

- Alchemy is about creating magic

- To create magic you must believe

- To create magic you must be able to imagine

- To create magic you must trust

- Initiating alchemy is a skill

- Cultivating a skill requires practice

- To ignite money alchemy you need imagination and enthusiasm

- Imagination and enthusiasm are a frequency, like a channel on a dial

- Alchemy is about connecting with the wizard within

- The wizard within is light hearted and fun

- The wizard within knows s/he can

- You are the wizard within

Money as Energy

- Money is both physical and non physical

- Money is Energy

- Money is Potential

- Money flows

- Money is everywhere

- Money needs direction and containment

- You can direct the flow of money

- You can contain money

- You are energy

- You and money are made of the same stuff

- You are the money

> *Money is congealed energy, and releasing it*
> *releases life's possibilities*
> Joseph Campbell

Money as Journey

- Making money is not an event
- Making money is a journey
- Making money is a process
- Making money is a destination

At the start of your money journey:

- You must know you are on a journey
- You must know where you are
- You must know where you are going
- To know where you are means to know who you are
- To know where you are going means to know who you want to become
- Who you want to become is a feeling
- That feeling is the destination of your money journey
- You are the source of your money journey
- You are the destination of your money journey
- You are the money journey

The only journey is the one within
Rainer Maria Rilke

Money as Process of Transformation

- Making money is a process of becoming

- Making money is a quest for changing self

- Wealth creation is a process of self transformation

- Wealth is a means of creating a new you

- To transform self you must change

- To change you must let go

- To change you must see yourself as you are

- To change you must acknowledge your shadow

- To change you must know who you want to become

- Who you want to become means feeling in a certain way

- Money is a mirror

- Money will make you more of who you are

- Being wealthy is a feeling

- The feeling of being wealthy is different for everyone

- To become wealthy you must connect to that feeling

- To become wealthy, you must be wealthy

Each entered the forest at a point he, himself, had chose,
where it was darkest and there was no path
from *Quest for the Holy Grail*

Money as Potential

- Money is Potential

- Potential needs direction, form and containment

- Your goal is your money destination

- To contain money you need a container

- Your container is your goal

- Your money container must be specific

- Your container represents your choice of destination or goal

- The container walls represent boundaries and parameters

- The container walls must be strong, yet flexible

- Money will be drawn to fill your container

- You must expand your container as your money needs expand

- You contain the money

- You contain many aspects of your life

- Your ability to contain will determine what is contained

- Your ability to contain reflects your ability to be

- You must increase your beingness to increase your container

- You are your money container

- You are the potential unfolding

Money as Relationship

Everything exists by virtue of relationship

- Everything is connected, everything is energy
- Money reflects your relationship with others
- Money reflects your relationship with self
- Money is a mirror
- You are in relationship with everything
- When you change one relationship, all your relationships change
- You are in relationship with money
- Relationships are a two-way process of give and take
- Money needs you in order for it to transform
- Money needs you in order to manifest
- Money is attracted to the magical and the extraordinary
- Your extraordinary dream will attract money to you

I think what we are seeking is an experience of being alive,
so that our life experiences on the purely physical plane,
will have resonances with our innermost being and reality,
so that we actually feel the rapture of being alive.'
Joseph Campbell

Money as Teacher

- Money is a teacher
- Money teaches what you most need to learn
- Money's lessons are many, amongst them:
  - **Generosity and Openness**
  - **Cycle of Give and Receive**
  - **Attention**
  - **Trust**
  - **Expansion and Containment**
  - **Respect**
  - **Simplicity**
- Money will reveal your lead so you can transform it to gold
- Money will mirror your expectations and resonance
- Money can guide you to your highest potential
- Through money you can discover the teacher within

Freedom consists not in refusing to recognise anything above us, but in respecting something which is above us; for by respecting it, we raise ourselves to it, and by our very acknowledgement, prove that we bear within ourselves what is higher, and are worthy to be on a level with it.

Goethe

Fabulous Feedback from Coaching Clients and Course Participants of Money Alchemy

The following are thank you letters and extracts from the feedback forms of participants of The Alchemy of Money courses. They are produced with permission and, where requested, the names have been changed. The feedback, however, remains unchanged, as do the professions of the participants.

I have clarified my life purpose! Kiki, you are a wonderful and inspiring teacher.

Denis Ginn – Professional photographer

Excellent. I thought that you did an amazing job combining many sources from your background and studies in an integrated programme.

What most amazed me was the depth and background of your knowledge. I was concerned that the workshop would be new-age airy fairy, but was so impressed with the groundedness of your resources. The latent power in what you presented is immeasurable.

Audrey Shuttle – Architect

I have had a complete shift – money moves like energy – is attracted to the extraordinary, fun and colourful – it is easy to access with the right mindset.

I got practical tools for radical change and achieving financial abundance plus understanding the principles behind this.

Various potential projects have emerged since the course too. A client confirmed a contract after 6 months of hedging.

Louise Sterling – Director & co-owner Edu-Write

It has expanded how I work with my business, how I focus my energy. It allowed me to focus on my business in a different way, I found it useful, motivating, inspiring, and really took a step to taking my business to the next level.

It is a chance to shift your own perceptions and attitudes about money – life changing.

Pat Strong – Business owner, Materials Development

I gained reassurance and deeper clarity around where I am regarding my mission in life; an attitude of questioning my attitude around exchange (monetary and otherwise); and several practical strategies to deal with various exchange and money related issues.

The course is about transforming patterns in life using money as a mirror.

Elisabeth Dostal – Futurist, Management Consultant & Business Owner

This workshop is a must. It will revolutionise your concept of money and its flow in your life.

More importantly, you will discover how you hinder money's manifestation in your life.

Dan Harwood – Businessman

I am now in control of money and not the other way round.

Dane Able – Hair salon owner

It shifted my concept of money and its relationship in my life as a processing tool. You clearly have a wealth of knowledge and experience in this field.

May Brown – Occupational counselling psychologist

I learnt that we are MAGICIANS in every sense. That it is GOOD to have big, wild dreams.

I LEFT COMPLETELY REFRESHED AND FULL OF ENERGY – FELT FANTASTIC, RESOLVED AND CLEAR!

Dr Diane Kerry – Scientist

My quote would be, 'Finding your elusive centre can be one's greatest challenge in life, the Alchemy of Money course helps you to continue the journey to attain it'. The course comes highly recommended and Kiki Theo is a skilled practitioner and process facilitator.

Petrina Roberts – Executive Director, NGO

A lot of fun. An eye-opener. Something you must approach with an open mind. Be prepared to realise completely new aspects of your life and yourself. Presented by a woman with life experience – if you name it, she has probably done it!

It has changed my perception of money ... possibly completely! I can't quite put my finger on it, but it doesn't seem to be an issue any more ... or certainly not like it seemed before!

Jon Smithfield – Naval Search & Rescue Co-Ordinator

I was inspired by the fact that you have made it happen and you shared your secrets.

The workshop is about accessing your inner power connected to unlimited potential and abundance. It gives you grounded tools to get in the money flow and encourages you to step into a real relationship with this energy instead of excuses that keep one stuck in lack.

The way to get your mind right before making money.

Gay French – Yoga teacher

Thank you for your guidance and support over the last few months. Your insights based on the spiritual as well as practical aspects of business have been very beneficial in facilitating an empowering process of growth. You provided a safe space for my dreams to find a voice and to become reality.

Al Winter – Occupational Therapist and Business Owner

I learnt that I cannot have what I want if I don't believe in the impossible.

Sharon Day – Business Owner

You really have a calling as a facilitator and I think you were excellent. It was very informative and practical so you can go away with tools and techniques to assist yourself in life. It was a matter of taking oneself out the left hand side of the brain (logic and practicality), and using the right hand side of the brain to solve problems and manifest all your dreams and desires.

Pam Short – Medical Sales

I realised that money is not 'a thing' as such, but a flow of energy.

I say to people that it is about changing your view of money and your thinking about money … it is about thinking about money as an energy flow … it is about learning a new meaning for the word 'intention' and then setting an intention. I tell them about the 3 rules and about having impossible dreams and that it is about learning new concepts which may seem airy-fairy but are very powerful if you put them into practice. I tell them that the course will teach them how to manifest anything they want in their lives.

Marilyn Krane – Computer Developer & Business Owner

Dear Kiki

My world is different since that day I picked up your flyer. Maybe I can explain it like this: One day we were standing in your garden after a coaching session and suddenly you were in awe about a beautiful butterfly passing by. How can I not think of you now when I see a butterfly?

Every time I mention your workshop to others, my explanation and perception of what it meant to me keep changing, keep growing. It assisted me immensely on my personal journey of self-discovery. Business-wise it provided me with the concept of building a container to hold and facilitate the flow of my money.

So the only 'fact' about you and your workshops I will ever be able to write about is this: Life Changing.

My warmest regards

Felicity Greenberg – Financial Planner

Dear Kiki

It's about a year since I attended your workshops. This past year has been filled with major good changes.

I was so stuck before, but the workshops have helped me tremendously.

What I have earned in the last 6 months equals what I earned in the 12 months before I attended your workshop.

A big thank you for what you do – please don't stop your workshops.

Sharon Day – Business Owner

A Wealthy New Beginning

Moving forward

I feel as if I have come to know you through these pages. I celebrate your courage in taking this journey. It is only the start. Keep practising. Keep imagining. Keep believing. And trust.

Whatever does not serve you, let it go. Don't make a big deal out of it. You don't have to go as far as cutting off your arm ... Just let it go.

Stay close to those who nourish your spirit. They are a gift. Celebrate! Today, if possible. Celebrate whatever you want. Celebrate alone, or celebrate with friends, but celebrate!

Connect with the Divine. That is the only true source of inspiration and guidance. Listen to the quiet voice within. This is only the beginning of the wealth journey. Very soon, you will need to know how to contain the wealth that is coming your way. You will need to fix any leaks and blocks to the money flow. You will need to transform obstacles, and take your money training to the next level. And for that, you will need the next book – *The Money Well*™. (What, you thought you'd skip the ads?)

The Money Well™

Having gone through the groundwork and preparation contained in this book, you will be ready to face the amazingly powerful processing contained in *The Money Well™ – How to contain wealth*. In this ground breaking holistic approach to transformation through money making, you will explore wealth, working with the metaphor of a container. Using a variety of creative and energetic tools you will reflect on the containment of various aspects of your life with the focus on wealth using the principles of containment as a guide. You will uncover and repair leaks and blocks in your wealth flow using *The Money Well™* Process and learn practical tools that will help you continue your wealth expansion and containment. *The Money Well™* energetic transformations are a unique and powerful way to fast forward on your wealth track.

As Oprah once said, 'It's not how much money you get to make, it's how much money you get to keep that's important.' And that, is what *The Money Well™* is all about.

I look forward to chatting to you again in *The Money Well™*. Meanwhile, I leave you with the following quotes and with my warmest wishes that you experience wealth, health, and happiness.

What we need, is more people who specialise in the impossible
Theodore Roethke

Only the impossible is worth doing
Dr Akong Tulku Rinpoche

You are an alchemist; make gold of that
William Shakespeare

Acknowledgements

There are many people I would like to thank for helping me arrive at this point in my life: My father, for leaving the doors of possibility open; my mother who helped me discover my inner strength and taught me the love of books; Martin de Chatillon, wonderful teacher and mentor, who introduced me to Jung, working with symbol, and who said that I should write; Allegra Taylor at Skyros who encouraged my writing further; Anthony Prolad who put me on the path; Mr Au, my first tai-chi teacher, who taught me about energy; Rob Nairn of the Kagyu lineage of Tibetan Buddhism, beloved teacher of meditation, who taught me how to work with the mind; the staff, teachers and participants of Skyros Holistic Holidays for facilitating a major shift (and providing a husband); Craig Wilkie, my fabulous business partner without equal, who has shared most of my wealth creation moments, and who was there from the beginning; Anne Schuster who has helped me hone my writing skills, and for the women's monthly writing group for keeping the writing faith through the years; the first readers of my book – Rose, Lana, Ginny, Maire, Riri, Shaun, Craig – for their insightful input; Maire Fisher for her warmth, enthusiasm, consistent encouragement, willingness and superb editing; Simone Redman for fabulous illustrations; Ginny Felling for keeping the energy clear in my life; Irma Stanley-Best, practitioner of directed pressure point technique and amazing healer, who helped me get my health back; all my clients and staff across time for their trust and support; and all the participants of the Alchemy of Money courses and coaching clients for their courage and for trusting me to facilitate their journey. Finally I would like to thank Alex and Sasha, the joys of my life, who teach me daily the great art of being human; and the love of my life Shaun, who holds the space for me to transcend, I love you.

Recommended Reading

The following books will be helpful to you on your wealth transformation journey.

The process of Creation and Manifestation

The Power of Intention: Learning to Co-create Your World Your Way – Dr Wayne W Dyer (Hay House, 2004)

Excuse Me, Your Life is Waiting: The Astonishing Power of Feelings – Lynn Grabhorn (Hampton Roads Publishing Co. Inc., 2003)

Transforming Self

The Secret of the Shadow: The Power of Owning Your Whole Story – Debbie Ford (Hodder Mobius, 2005)

The Alchemy of the Heart – Reshad Feild (Element Books Ltd, 1990)

Transforming Mind

Tranquil Mind: An Introduction to Buddhism and Meditation – Rob Nairn (Kairon Press, 2004)

Diamond Mind: A Psychology of Meditation – Rob Nairn (Kairon Press, 2001)

The Tibetan Art of Serenity: How to Conquer Fear and Gain Contentment – Christopher Hansard (Hodder Mobius, 2008)

Transformational Processing

Life Choices, Life Changes: The Art of Developing Personal Vision through Imagework – Dina Glouberman (Thorsons – Harper Collins, 1999)

The Tibetan Art of Positive Thinking – Christopher Hansard (Hodder Mobius)

Principles of Success

The Dip: A little book that teaches you when to quit (and when to stick) – Seth Godin (Piatkus, 2007)

The Greatest Salesman in the World – Og Mandino (Bantam Books, 1995)
All the principles for success, sales, marketing, and wealth creation are contained in this very small, very old little book – a classic must read.

Other

Eat, Pray, Love: One Woman's Search for Everything – Elizabeth Gilbert (Bloomsbury, 2007)
A novel based on the author's real life journey of transformation. Not just chick-lit.

The Millionaire next Door: The Surprising Secrets of America's Wealthy – T J Stanley & W D Danko (Longstreet Press). A look at real wealth.

I dedicate the merit of this work to our enlightenment and the enlightenment of all beings.